was provided by the

WITHD

516368

FOOTBALL AND THE SINGLE MAN

Football and the Single Man

by PAUL HORNUNG

as told to AL SILVERMAN

DOUBLEDAY & COMPANY, INC.
Garden City, New York
1965

Library of Congress Catalog Card Number 65–23789
Copyright © 1965 by Paul Hornung and Al Silverman
All Rights Reserved
Printed in the United States of America
First Edition

For Mom

"We all call him the Golden Boy because everything he does seems to turn out all right."

—JOE DOYLE, South Bend *Tribune*

Contents

PART III

PART IV

Part I

1. EVERY DAY IS DERBY DAY

Waiting at St. Vincent's Hospital to have the pinched nerve in my neck X-rayed, I met my true love and my true love said to me, "What is it this time, the neck or the head?"

Her name is Sister Viola and she is in charge of the emergency room at St. Vincent's Hospital in Green Bay and she is one of the beautiful people of this world. She has grieved for me in my small triumphs, and when I missed five field goals against the Baltimore Colts, she phoned me and said, "Don't you feel bad." And her call made me feel not quite so bad.

Now she was standing before me in her severe white habit with her thick severe eyeglasses unable to hide those huge dark eyes, eyes that were mixed with concern and merriment.

"You've had that before, haven't you?" she said.

"Yes."

"Next time," she said, "you let them have the ball."

It had happened the day before—in the third quarter against the Detroit Lions. Cutting into the hole, I tripped over the feet of my Green Bay Packer teammate, Forrest Gregg. I flipped over in the air, like a dolphin, and came right down on my head.

Baby, I said to myself, you've had it today. I could feel

the pain right down to my spine, the same kind of pain that hit me in the championship game in 1960. That time I immediately lost all control of my arm. Many months after, in fact, I would find myself shaving and shaking the shaving cream and the can would fall out of my hand. I'd be drinking a glass of water and I'd feel the glass almost slip out of my hand. And that's just the way it felt as I flipped over Gregg and I was out of the game.

And now Sister Viola was noticing me grimace as I tried to twist my neck and she said, "Would you like a halter to sleep with?"

"No," I said, "I got me a little blonde to sleep with."

She put her hands on her hips and shook her head and bravely ignored my blasphemies.

"You played a real good game yesterday. We were so nervous." In addition to everything else, she is, like most people of this city, a Green Bay Packer fan, and she became more solicitous by the moment.

"Anything we can do for you?"

"Yes," I said. "This girl said to me yesterday, 'What do I do, I'm pregnant?'"

"You should get hung up," Sister Viola said sweetly. "A traction hook-up will be good for your neck."

"Will you give me two, Sister, one for my fiancée?"

"Oh, Paul." The tone suggested that I was incurable.

"Oh, Sister Viola," I pressed on. "You know, I'd like to open a bar some day and make you chief cocktail waitress."

"I'd serve holy water," the Sister spoke firmly. "You need something to calm your nerves."

I said, "I know what I need. I need a couple of wives, that's what I need. What I'll do is I'll marry out of the Church the first time and if that doesn't work, I'll be able to get a divorce and marry into the Church."

"Isn't he something?" Sister Viola said. "Isn't he something?" And after I had my X-rays and was ready to leave, she pressed two books in my hand. One was called *Three Minutes a Day*, by Father James Keller. The other was *The Quest of Honor*, by Boyd Barrett. Both were inspirational types and I got the message.

"I'll read them, I promise, Sister."

And as I was leaving she called out after me, "You be more careful," and I thought to myself, if I had been more careful I wouldn't be hurt. But you can't be more careful to play this game.

I stepped outside marveling at the weather, so unusual for Green Bay in mid-November. The temperature this November 9, 1964 was sixty-eight and the sky was a beckoning golf sky and I wished I could enjoy it. The weekend had been a fine swinging weekend, a winning one. We had won a football game, a lot of my friends had come in, and that's the way it should always be in Green Bay during the football season.

The tension for that Detroit game had begun building on Tuesday. It always begins building on Tuesday. It's like building a sand castle on the beach. You keep pouring on the sand, pouring it on and pouring it on, until you think you've got something and then, all of a sudden, it starts to crumble and disintegrate and you have to start practically all over again. That's what we do from Tuesday to Sunday preparing for a football game.

Sunday night and Monday is our free time after the game. That's the time when we just let the sand lay there. Those are the nights, win or lose, we like to go out and just have a good time. Those are the nights we like to have a few beers and get with the guys and party and let down our hair, turn up the juke box, and if you want to holler and scream and sing and dance, why not? In the old days in Green Bay

when we were losing, people would see us out having dinner and having a cocktail and that was a sin to them. They
thought, well they should be home in a corner somewhere.
But nobody can live that way. When we were losing, one of
the ways we kept up our spirits in fact was going out and
having a good time and getting our minds off it as well as
we could. Naturally, when you win, everything's fine.

So the work begins on Tuesday—Coach always says you
should be ready to play on Tuesday—and everyone is very
relaxed and loose. And then Wednesday you start getting a
little bit more serious and put in what you're going to do
that Sunday and start studying it; and then Thursday it
starts wearing on your nerves a little bit and on Friday it
hits you.

So it helps settling into a routine, and that's what we do
beginning on Friday, and that's what we did the Friday before the Detroit game.

Friday morning practices are mostly concerned with running your draw plays and your screen plays, screens to your
halfbacks and fullbacks, and a short fifteen-minute drill on
passing, and just a day, actually, to get sharp on your passing
game and your draws and screens. And after practice, naturally, we look at the movies again of the team we're going
to play that Sunday. And this Friday we finished at one and
we went to the Spot—Max McGee, Ron Kramer, and myself
—for lunch.

That afternoon, as we do every Friday afternoon in Green
Bay, we went to the movies. The fellow who runs the show
downtown is a real good friend of ours. We went in and the
balcony was closed up and Ron and Max and I were the
only three guys in the balcony and so we could really relax.
The movie Friday night before the Detroit game was something called *Pajama Party*, and we enjoyed it.

Friday night I had some running back and forth to do.

First I went to the airport to pick up an old friend of mine, Don Forst. Don and I went to high school together in Louisville and he came in for the weekend. Later, I went to get my Louisville partner, Bill King, and his wife, Doris. Later that night I picked up another friend—Pat Fontecchio, who owns a supper club in northern Wisconsin. I made arrangements to have dinner with all my friends Saturday night.

Saturday morning, the ritual continued. Pat Martin, who is my best friend in Green Bay, came over to the house that Max, Ron, and I rented. He had breakfast with us the Saturday before the Detroit game as he does every Saturday we're home, and we played cribbage. Then we went over to the field, which is close to the house, for a short practice session. We did thirty minutes of calisthenics and loosening-up and a five-minute goal-line drill.

Back at the house we settled into our routine. Saturday is a good day for watching television. Green Bay is a small town and after eight or nine years, you can go through the town maybe in three months and be in every place. So after eight or nine years you find yourself looking at television. I can remember in 1963 during my sabbatical (the year Alex Karras of Detroit and myself were suspended for betting on football games) I watched television maybe five times the whole year. In 1964 I could almost tell you every program, Monday through Saturday.

So we sat in the living room, Max, Ron, and I, and watched the college football game. In years past, Jimmy Taylor used to bring his daughter over for the game and we'd sit around and watch. And now Jimmy's got a little boy and he keeps him busy around the house now. It's just a little bit too much to bring them both over—the little one is such a tiger.

The Saturday before the Detroit game was a little different, though, because we have a lot of close friends on the

Lions. Terry Barr went to Michigan with Ron and he came over with a couple of his teammates—Wayne Walker and Gary Lowe. And of course, Quinny, Bill Quinlan, came over. Quinny played five years with the Packers and we're all close friends. We could have held the game right here on Saturday, right in the house. It was a real nice afternoon—having a beer and watching the game. And Quinlan was as outrageous as ever.

"You know what they ought to do tomorrah," he said in his booming Boston Irish voice. "Instead of the captains maarching out for the coin-toss before the game, they ought to let Hornung and Karras do it." The reference of course was to our suspension and I came right back at him.

"I saved your life, baby!" I hollered. "And don't you forget it! I SERVED TIME FOR YOU."

That night was just an enjoyable evening. We went to the Spot for dinner, which I think is the best restaurant in Green Bay. Bill and Doris King were there, Pat Fontecchio, Don Forst, and Pat Martin and his lovely wife, Mary Ellen. I had no date because I don't like going out the night before a game. I can't go out on Friday or Saturday night and play on Sunday. It's a superstition with me. When I was in high school I was very superstitious. One night I scored twenty points in a basketball game and the next time we played I wore the same shirt, sweater, shoes, and shorts—the whole thing. I'm not like that any more, except when it comes to going out before a game. I have done it actually and I have had bad luck when I have done it. Every time I've ever done it, I've always gotten hurt or something like that.

And I picked up the check for dinner, which I love to do. I think it goes back to when I was young. I'd gone to a lot of nice places only with my mother and my uncle and they weren't flashy or anything. But when I was at Notre Dame

I got squired around quite a little bit; and now I wanted to be the squire and do things for people.

Still, I think I'm a little hypocritical about money. I go out and have a few drinks and there'll be dinner for twelve and I'll pick up the check. And then again I'll need a white cashmere coat—really need it—and I won't buy it if I don't think it's worth what they're asking. It's a different atmosphere and a different set of responsibilities. Dinner with friends is one thing. Going out for a coat is another. It's like if someone handed me a million dollars, I'd want to invest it. But if somebody handed me a million dollars and said you have two years to spend it, I'd go do it. I'd go to Europe and blow it in two years. But that would be two years I'd never forget the rest of my life.

Anyway, I took my fantasies home with me early that Saturday night. We have to be in at eleven on Saturdays and I was in on time and watched television, and that was it.

Sunday morning the ritual continued. I got up and went to Mass and then it was breakfast at 10 A.M. at the Jesse Whittentons. Jesse plays defensive back for us and his wife Joanne makes steak and eggs for everybody. I don't eat steak and eggs. I just have coffee and toast, and that's what I had.

We arrived at the stadium about 11:15 and lay around and got taped and talked and tried to stay as loose as we could. I've always been considered a very loose ballplayer, but I'm maybe not quite as loose as a lot of people think. Bart Starr is always kidding me about it. He says, "Before a game, I'm very nervous and shook up and I look at you and it's just unbelievable how loose you look and you can kid and talk and nothing seems to bother you." But, naturally, it does bother me. Wanting to win so much is what bothers me. I'm not the kind of guy who's going to holler and scream, you know, be a real hip-hip-hooray kind of guy. Whether you holler or scream it's not going to mean one

damn thing unless you win, unless you get the job done.
And that's what always bothers me—wanting to get the job
done—and that's how the tension hits me.

Then Coach Lombardi came in and talked to us. We had
a 4–4 record so far and Detroit was in second place at 5–2–1
and Coach told us we still had a good shot at second place.
"You're the loose ones now," he told us. "You have nothing
to lose and everything to gain. So go out and play with *reckless abandon.*" That's one of Vince Lombardi's favorite
phrases and what he means is that the team that blocks the
hardest and tackles the hardest is going to come out on top.
The pros are all taught to play with reckless abandon. You
play reckless football, you play with abandon, but you play
with intelligence, too. And when you have a chance to make
a tackle, you better make it. In college you might be graded
an "A" on extreme effort; you might miss the tackle and the
coach says, "Great hustle." Hustle's wonderful in the pros,
don't get me wrong, but you just better make sure you get
that tackle or all the hustle goes for nothing. It's not too
much to give 110 per cent when you're playing, Coach says,
because the actual playing time for an offensive player is
about thirteen minutes, the actual time while the plays are
going on. And out of those twelve or thirteen minutes' playing time, you can accrue so much popularity and receive
such fantastic salary for doing it, you have to give as much
to football as it's gonna give to you. Those are Vince Lombardi's ideals. He's a very, very intelligent man and I think
every Packer ballplayer thinks the way he does.

And the game itself.

We took the opening kickoff and went seventy-three
yards in thirteen plays and I handled the ball only once,
taking a screen pass for four yards. Jimmy Taylor and Bart
Starr did the heavy work, Jimmy running and Bart running

and passing, and we really moved. I kicked the extra point and it was 7–0.

We held them and took the ball on our sixteen. On the first play Bart called for the fullback toss play right side sweep. On it, the right tackle and tight end block down on the defensive end. I try to veer out and block the linebacker. The split end comes in and blocks the safetyman, and the pulling guard knocks out the defending halfback.

It worked perfectly. I got inside the linebacker at a real fine angle and just cut him out of the play. Everyone made their blocks and Jimmy just ran away, went down the sidelines and pushed the last defender into the end zone. It was his longest run ever and, as it turned out, the longest scrimmage run all year in the NFL.

In the second quarter we moved down to the Detroit forty yard line, they held, and I came in to try a field goal. Up to this one, I had only kicked six out of twenty-one field goal attempts in 1964, and I didn't know what was the matter. I had gone back and looked at those films of 1960, '61, '62, of myself kicking and I couldn't see anything drastically different than I was doing. The steps were the same, my follow-through was the same, but the ball wasn't going between the goal posts. I was like a golfer caught in a slump and I didn't know what to do and Coach said I was pressing and I guess, naturally, I was pressing. I was trying to get the thing through there and the more you miss the more you start thinking. But I wasn't pressing the moment I was kicking the ball. It was afterward, the fact that the thing was missed and trying to figure out what was wrong.

So I went out there thinking of the fifteen out of twenty-one missed so far and wondering if this would be another miss. And the ball was snapped back to Bart, who is one of the best in the league at holding it, and he placed the strings in front and I went into my two-step—right, left, kick—and

at the moment of impact I knew that it would be far enough
and accurate enough. And it was. I felt very good, naturally.

After the game Vince Lombardi told a writer, "I was very
happy for Hornung and the team. . . . I think everybody
was saying a silent prayer for him before he made that first
one."

I kicked two more and missed one forty-one yarder by a
matter of inches and we won the game, 30–7, and even that
pinched nerve in my neck and the pain didn't feel quite so
bad. We won and I had played a pretty good game. You
know, I've played a good ball game when we lost and felt
real bad about it, and I've played a bad ball game when we
won and felt real bad about it. And, naturally, the best way
to feel is to play a good ball game when you win, and that's
paramount. And that's how I felt as I got ready to party.

A very nice fellow in town, Bob Cowles, and his wife, had
a big dinner party at his house and everyone came—all my
friends who were in for the weekend, and even some of the
Detroit players. Their flight had been canceled because of
fog so they got to swing with us.

And swing we did. The party continued late into the night
at our house. Some of those Lion players—they rummaged
in my drawers and made themselves comfortable in my
Bermuda shorts. And it was a long, enjoyable night and I
never did get to sleep, and later Bill Quinlan took my car
and I didn't see it or him again. I had to pick up the car at
the airport the next day and dump a load of used spareribs
off the front seat.

I hadn't thought about the car Sunday night, of course.
Then, mostly, I was thinking of just letting off steam; the
tension and hurts were forgotten as the music played and
my girl and I danced into the night. Speaking of girls, which
I will be doing quite a bit, the question has been asked of
me, do I like girls or football best? I like girls quite a lot. I

like to have fun, as I did that Monday with Sister Viola at the hospital, and as she did with me. I've enjoyed the reputation, I can't say that I haven't, even though I think it's been exaggerated. I've enjoyed being called "The Golden Boy." It's helped me. You know, you're only yourself and if you try to be anybody else you'd be ridiculous.

Friends of mine back in Louisville say, "Every day is Derby day for Paul Hornung." Kentucky Derby day in Louisville is the biggest day of the year for us and I love it and look forward to it. And in a sense I'd like every day of my life to be like that one day. And in a sense, they have. I don't have any regrets about my life. Everything I've wanted, I've gotten, and the only real bad thing was the suspension. I've always liked a good time. I like good food. I like good restaurants. I like pretty girls. I like driving a Cadillac. I like going first class. And football has given me this opportunity. And if I didn't keep up with football, didn't continue to give it the best I have, the first-class stuff would turn into a ride on a coach.

Besides, the plain fact is I like football very much. I think that over and above what the sportswriters like to think, that I'm a little bit more conscientious about football than actually realized. I think that still I would rather score a touchdown on a particular day than make love to the prettiest girl in the United States.

And the idea of not being able to play football, not being *allowed* to play, is what hit me the hardest when the world fell in on me in 1963.

2. THE BIGGEST DECISION OF MY LIFE

On the ninth day of January 1963, at ten-thirty in the morning, I left the Plaza Hotel and headed for the one place in New York City I felt I had to be—St. Patrick's Cathedral.

I was in a turmoil. Pete Rozelle's words kept ringing in my mind. "We have reason to believe that you have been betting on football games. . . . We'd like to have you take a lie detector test. . . . You know, you don't have to take a lie detector test, but we'd like you to. . . . Think it over awhile. If you want to take a lie detector test, come back and tell me."

Earlier in our meeting Pete Rozelle, the Commissioner of the National Football League, had asked me straight out, "Have you bet on football games?" And I had said no.

And now I had a couple of hours around New York to decide what to do. It was probably the biggest decision I've had to make in my life and I was more shook up than I've ever been.

I don't shake up easily, you know. I've always been easy-going, cocksure of myself in anything I've ever done. I've always made decisions quick. I've never had to say, you know, I'll give you my decision in a week or so, or something like that—unless it's a business deal and I know what I'm going to do anyway, and maybe I'm just playing him along for a bigger piece or something. But I never have been slow in making up my mind to do something. Like when I was in the Army at Fort Riley, Kansas, on a Thursday afternoon and I said, "Gee, I'd like to be in Los Angeles." So naturally, I'd get a pass and be there that night. I wouldn't make plans *two weeks* before going to L.A.

But this was a little different. This was a real serious situation. I said to myself, Well, baby, you're on your own now, you're really on your own now.

So I went into church and said a few prayers and everything and thought of the alternatives.

Number one, I didn't have to take the lie detector test.

Number two, they didn't know Barney Shapiro was the only guy I ever bet with.

Now if I wanted to lie, I could say, no, I don't want to take the lie detector test, and I probably could have lied out of it and might have gotten away with it. I don't know if I would have or not. What could they do? I thought there was a fifty-fifty chance. And me being the way I am, I like better odds than that.

But there was more to it than that. I figured now I'm playing around with my life—my life in professional athletics. And everything I've done up to now could very easily go down the drain. I thought, well if I'm truthful and honest about it, maybe I'll get a break. That's all I could ask.

It was a cold, damp day in New York, just the way I felt. It's one of the few times I've ever come to New York that I wasn't looking for a date. I didn't care about looking in the little black book for numbers. I had another phone call to make.

I left St. Patrick's, found a telephone booth, and called Pete Rozelle at the National Football League office. I said, "I want to take the lie detector test, Pete. I want to make a full confession-type of statement . . . that I was gambling."

And he said that would be fine, and now it was all over for me.

When I was a kid in Louisville I did what most kids do. I played a little poker, I played a little pinball machine, I pitched nickels and dimes with my friends. Just little childhood sidelights is all they were.

When I got older, after college especially, I became very fond of horse races. I love horses and, of course, I come from horse country. I've always enjoyed the times at home like we'd go down to Keeneland in beautiful Lexington, and we'd play golf, then go to the races, and have lunch and dinner. It was just a real nice day, and I've always enjoyed it since college.

And Louisville, you know, is a ramblin'-gamblin' horse racing town. There is nowhere better in the world than Louisville at Derby time. My friends come in and we go to the races maybe four days in a row and the Kentucky Derby is the climax and that's it—one big ball.

Everything I've ever done since I've been in athletics, even in high school, has been exaggerated. If I was at the window betting twenty dollars, somebody would say he saw me at the fifty-dollar window. I'm not saying I wasn't ever at the fifty-dollar window, but I was never at the fifty-dollar window as much as they said I was. I didn't go to the races to try and make a living, you know.

I've always been more of an *impulsive* gambler than a compulsive gambler. If I'm around it, I have the impulse to do it. If I'm up in Green Bay during the season, I have no compulsion to gamble. I would never be the one to say, "Gee, I sure would like to get up a poker game now." But if somebody said, "We'll get a poker game going," then, naturally, Max McGee and I would be there.

But I never bet a football game in my life until 1959 and that started after I had met Barney Shapiro.

Barney Shapiro is a man of about forty-five now and he's a real big football fan. I mean he likes to bet football, you know. He doesn't bet on the horse races, he doesn't bet on baseball or basketball or anything, but he just likes football.

Barney is not a professional bettor, don't get me wrong. He'd maybe bet $500 on each game—maybe a $500 parlay on a couple of teams or something. But he wasn't betting $5,000 or anything. He wasn't betting, in other words, over and beyond his means where it was hurting him. He wasn't taking any food from his family or anything. As far as I know, he could always afford to bet.

I met Barney at a restaurant in San Francisco when I was out there for the East-West game in December of my senior year at Notre Dame. He lived in San Mateo and we were working out close by in San Jose and a couple of the other ballplayers and myself went out to his house for dinner once or twice.

At the time Barney owned the B & B Novelty Company, a coin machine business. Later he moved to Las Vegas where he set up a pinball machine, games, and other type machines.

We became friends. In the summer of 1957, just before I was to report to the college All-Star camp for the game against the NFL champions, I went out to Vegas as Barney's guest and I stayed there and lost $400 or $500 on the slot machines and dice and I had a showgirl friend there and it was a fine time. I love Vegas, you know. It has great shows, a fun town.

In 1957, my first year with the Packers, Barney called me often. And then it wasn't anything, you know. A couple of times he just called to see how I was. We were just friends. I still regard him as a friend. Naturally, I can't be around him now, but if I was ever in trouble and needed a friend, I know I could count on him.

Maybe I was naïve, but I never felt I was doing anything wrong those first two years talking to Barney and sometimes giving him my opinion about ball games. He'd call up and say, "How you doing?" I'd say, "Oh, pretty good." He'd say, "What do you feel about the game? Are you all ready?" And I'd say, yes.

Then, in 1959 after Coach Lombardi came to the Packers and we began to develop a pretty good club, I started to bet.

The first time was in one of our exhibition games in 1959. Barney called me and we talked awhile. He asked me the usual information.

"How do you feel?"

"I feel fine," I said.

He said, "What do you think? You're eight-point favorites."

And I said, "I think it's a good bet. I think we'll win."

Then we talked a little longer and, all of a sudden, strictly on an impulse, I said to Barney, "Well, bet me a hundred."

So I made maybe eight or nine bets in 1959. I didn't bet on our games all the time, and I never asked Barney what he was betting. That was his business. I didn't care what he was betting.

I think there were two reasons I started to bet. One, just for pure kicks. Two, when it looked like I might make the Pro Bowl I wanted to have some walking-around money on the Coast. I liked to have a good time there.

The Pro Bowl game, matching the all-stars of the Eastern Conference against the all-stars of the Western Conference, is played in Los Angeles every January, right after the season. At that time we got $600 for playing in the game, $800 if we won, and that weekend cost me about $1500. I had a swinging time that week. You know, Los Angeles is an expensive town. You start taking a fiancée out. You're going to four night clubs, catching four shows and having dinner every night, and a party in the afternoon. We'd end up with a reservation every night to see Stan Kenton at the Crescendo night club. His is one of my favorite bands. Then the Treniers were in town and those are my boys. I always used to get up and sing with them. I know all their routines and they even offered me a job when I was suspended.

I remember the fellow I was staying with at the time, Bill George of the Chicago Bears, telling a writer that he had roomed all week with Paul Hornung's suitcase. Bill told me, "I don't mind taking your messages, you know, but why don't you come around once in a while?"

Couldn't. Too busy.

The game went well. We beat the East, 38–21. I scored a touchdown, kicked a field goal, and set a scoring record for the Pro Bowl with fourteen points.

I must have set a spending record, too. I spent all I had made that year betting on games. Barney had held it in escrow for me until I got out there.

That was the one and only year I ever made anything betting on football. After that, I just about broke even. I'd get ahead in the exhibition season and have a cushion going into the season, and I never would get behind. But I never got ahead, either.

I would bet two or three hundred a game. The biggest bet I ever made was $500 and that was a college game. It was the Wisconsin-Ohio State game in 1961 and Ohio State was favored by twelve points. The Wisconsin guy threw a touchdown pass as the gun went off and Ohio State won, 30–21. I lost that bet.

I think I was just average as a picker. The run-of-the-mill guy on the street could probably pick just as many games as

I could. It always seemed funny to me that everybody thinks, you know, that pro football players would be the greatest pickers in the world.

During my suspension I spoke to a lot of quarterback clubs around the country. And at a lot of those meetings, there would come a time when they would give out a $50 check to the guy who picked the most winners in the week's football pool. Of course it was a beautiful opening for me, being on suspension. They'd say, "Here is Charlie Brown, the winner this week in the pool. He picked twenty-four out of twenty-eight." And I always got up and congratulated that particular guy and I'd say—"You did a helluva lot better than I did, I'll tell you that."

All the while, before the whole thing blew sky-high, Barney kept calling me a couple of times a week and sometimes I'd call him.

I went along in my innocence figuring I was doing no wrong. You know, I've always said that you can second-guess yourself when you look back on it after it's over with. Of course, you should realize the pitfalls, realize the severity of it. But I never really did. I simply forgot that a player has an obligation to the sport and to the public. To me, it was just a nonchalant wager that I didn't think would be serious enough to worry about.

Then, in August of 1962, I knew it was a lot more serious than I had ever dreamed.

Paragraph Eleven of the National Football League players' contract is probably the most important clause in our contract, save for the one that spells out our pay. Paragraph Eleven is so important that a club regulation states: "Players must familiarize themselves with Paragraph Eleven of their contract." And the rule is posted in every team's dressing room.

Here is the guts of Paragraph Eleven:

> Player acknowledges the right and power of the Commissioner of the National Football League (a) to fine and suspend (b) to fine and suspend for life, indefinitely and/or (c) to cancel the contract of, any player who accepts a bribe or who agrees to throw or fix a game or who, having knowledge of the same, fails to report an offered bribe or an attempt to throw or fix a game, or who bets on a game, or who is guilty of any conduct detrimental to the welfare of the National Football League or to professional football. . . .

Every year since I have been in professional football, the Commissioner of the NFL has come around in the preseason and spelled out Paragraph Eleven for us. He would say, "Just abide by the rules and watch out for your associations." On August 25, 1962, we were in Milwaukee to play an exhibition game with the Chicago Bears, and Commissioner Pete Rozelle addressed the whole team on the subject. Afterwards, he came over to me.

"Can you have coffee with me, Paul?"

I said sure.

We spent about fifteen minutes together in the coffee shop and in that time Pete asked if I knew two men—Abe Samuels and Gil Beckley.

I told Pete all I knew. Abe Samuels was a friend of mine from Chicago who owns a duplicating machine company. Abe loves Notre Dame and I met him while I was playing. I know Abe bets on games but he never did call me, never did ask me anything, and I never did bet with Abe.

I know Gil Beckley, too. He lived in Miami and used to come to the Derby every year and I told Pete I had met Gil and had dinner with him during the year, but I never talked to Beckley during the season, and I certainly never talked to him about betting or anything like that.

That's all Pete asked me, whether I knew those guys, and then he said, "You're going to have to watch yourself. You're going to have to watch your associations. You have to be extra careful, Paul," he said, "because you're a bachelor and some people are always anxious to shoot down people in prominence."

He also said he thought it would be best if I didn't associate with Samuels or Beckley. I told Pete that Abe had wanted me to go into business with him right after the season, to open a franchise in Louisville, and he said it was all right but that he just didn't want me to get involved in any gambling with him.

And Barney Shapiro's name never came up.

I left Pete kind of shaken. For the first time in my life I started thinking about the consequences of my betting. And when the season started, I quit betting.

Barney was calling me still, but now I was getting scared talking to him on the telephone. Naturally, he was a friend of mine and I couldn't say, "Well, I can't talk to you any more." He would call and I would just say, "I think we're gonna win." What else could I say? We only lost one game that year.

But finally I did tell him I was scared and I said, "Barney, maybe you better not call me any more." And he said okay, and he stopped calling.

Then, early in January, right after the end of the season, after we had won our second straight NFL championship, I went out to California to work on the ads for the Jantzen company. The Pro Bowl game was the thirteenth so it was a chance to work and see the game (I hadn't made the team) and to be with my buddies.

On Tuesday, January 8, I went out to dinner with Bart Starr and his wife, Jim Taylor and his wife, Jerry Kramer and Barbara. We were having a fine time, and then I got a message to call Pete Rozelle immediately.

I called him at his home and he was terse over the phone. He said, "When can you come to New York? I'd like to talk to you. It's important."

Naturally, I had an idea what it was all about and I was a little worried and I hopped a night plane and was in New York the next morning, and at 10 A.M. I was meeting with Pete and a lawyer in their suite at the Plaza.

The first thing Pete did, he ran through a long list of names, and he asked me if I knew these people. And the only two I knew were Abe Samuels and Gil Beckley. There was one name on the list I was supposed to have been friends with and I never saw him in my life—never even heard about him. I found out later he was head of the Mafia in Chicago.

And then Pete came out about my betting and asked if I would take a lie detector test, and that's when I headed for St. Patrick's.

After talking to Pete, I went to this office building on West Forty-second Street. It was a real quiet place. There was a psychologist waiting for me, and an investigator from the NFL, and I wasn't even told their names. I felt like I was in espionage. I felt like James Bond.

I started hesitatingly at first; it was like I had to warm up. But then it poured out. I told them everything. I told about betting. I told about Barney Shapiro, whose name had never come up. I told them I had never bet with Abe Samuels or anybody except Barney. I told them everything there was to tell and they took it all down and afterward that NFL investigator told Pete he had felt sick for me and had been convinced completely.

And when I was finished, I talked to Rozelle on the telephone again. "I'll be in touch with you in a few days," he said. "Please keep this in strictest confidence." Then he said, "You can tell your mother if you want."

I said, "I'd rather not tell her."

I went back to Louisville shaken and troubled but relieved to have it off my chest, and I just waited.

In a few days Pete Rozelle called. He said, "Paul, I just don't know what to do. You know, I've always thought a lot of you."

Maybe he had. I had always gotten along well with Pete. But he had his job to do and it was a tough decision for him. He had to do something.

He said, "Now I guess you're wondering what avenues I have to follow."

"That's right," I said.

"Well, it could either be a reprimand, or it could be a fine and a reprimand, or a suspension." He said, "I don't know what to do. I've got to talk to a lot of other people. It's going to be a little while before it will come out in the papers, but you'll know about it before we make a statement."

The next three months were the longest months of my life. Every time the phone rang, I figured this was it. And I couldn't keep it to myself. Did you ever try to keep a secret? Did you ever try to keep something that weighed on your mind? You have to tell somebody. I don't know what it is. You've got to talk about it. I would have been a nervous wreck. I got nervous, anyway.

So I told Mom first. I certainly didn't want her to hear it from anyone else.

One day I said, "Mom, I want to talk to you." And I told her everything. I told her I had made some bets on games. I told her that I had done nothing wildly wrong, that I had never bet against my team. I kept looking at Mom and finally I said, "Now don't break up over something; don't let this get you down." And I knew she wouldn't, not in front of me.

And she said, "We've gone through a lot of rough spots all our life. Growing up is pretty hard, Paul, and you've been awfully fortunate all your life and if the good Lord has handed you something like this, you have to accept it."

And later I told my partner, Bill King. We had formed a partnership early in January, Productions Unlimited, and I was helping him promote sports shows and things like that. So I told Bill and I told my Uncle Henry, and I told my man at Jantzen's. I felt I had to because they had half a million dollars worth of advertisements tied up with me.

And those were the only people who knew, and every day it was waiting, waiting, waiting. And sleep came hard. Usually, you know, when I hit that bed, I don't move. But Mom said I did a lot of moving around those nights.

Then it was Wednesday, April 17, the one day I will specifically remember all my life. It was about ten in the morning and I was at my office with Bill King. And Mom got a call at her office. It was somebody from Pete Rozelle's office and they said they were trying to reach Paul. Then Pete himself got on the phone, and my mother didn't waste any formalities.

She said, "Is it bad, Mr. Rozelle?"

"Well, I'd rather not say, Mrs. Hornung. I'd better talk to Paul."

"I can understand that," my Mom said. "I'll get hold of Paul and have him call you."

Afterwards, Pete said he had choked up talking to my mother and had trouble getting the words out.

Then I got the call from Mom. She said, "I think there's news from New York. Mr. Rozelle wants you to call him."

Bill King drove me home and Mom was there when I got there. Bill went back to his office and I went into my room and sat on the bed and called New York. And my mother just stood there, in the doorway.

The first thing Pete said was, "We're going to release the news today. I'll tell you that you're not the only one involved. There are others."

I said, "I don't care about the others, Pete, what about me."

He said, "Well, I have to do something with you because of this gambling. We have to indefinitely suspend you." I was stunned. I could think of nothing to say.

He continued, "Your conduct will be watched in the following months. I will have to make some kind of re-evaluation of your case early in 1964."

I must have looked pretty dazed because Mom was looking at me with tears in her eyes.

"There's nothing else I can do," Pete was saying. "I know how bad you must feel. But under the circumstances, that's what has to be done. I hope you'll take it like a man."

I hung up the receiver and Mom said to me, "Is it bad, honey?"

"Yes, it's very bad. I've been suspended."

And now she started to cry and I would have cried, too, if I could have.

3. A STRANGE SABBATICAL

A few minutes later Bill King came back to the apartment and Mom made us sandwiches and we sat around and talked. Bill said, "Well, the first thing you better do is get your story ready."

I said, "I don't have a story I can get ready. I was wrong and that's all there is to it."

"I understand," Bill said, "but you're still going to have to make a statement to reporters. I tell you what, let's go play golf."

Bill figured we'd have some privacy at the country club and that I would have time to think out properly what I wanted to say, so I agreed to go to the club. But first I had two phone calls to make.

The first one was to Green Bay, to Coach Lombardi.

One of my big regrets in this whole mess was that I waited until the last minute to tell Coach about it. It hurt him to find out the way he did. I think if I had it all to do over (what am I saying!) I would have called him and sought his advice; I think he could have helped me.

Coach knew why I was calling; Pete Rozelle must have notified him in advance. So he wasn't surprised at what I was saying but he did say he was very hurt and embarrassed and disappointed that I hadn't talked to him about it.

I said, "I've let you down, I know I have, and all I can say is I'm sorry." And I was and there wasn't anything else I could say and Coach said, "You know I'm hoping you get reinstated next year and I don't want you reporting at any 250 pounds. So keep in shape and keep your nose clean and watch who you go around with and don't get in any more trouble, for heaven's sake."

I hung up feeling better already. Then I called Jim Rathbun of Jantzen's. I told him I had been suspended indefinitely. I told him I wanted Jantzen to be the first to know so they could do what they feel they ought to. So Jim said naturally he'd have to talk to other people in the company and that he would call me back as soon as they had made a decision.

Now I began to feel real down. I began to worry and wonder how the public would accept me. At this point I just didn't know what the public reaction would be.

So Bill and I went out to the golf course at our club, the Audubon Country Club, and I played a lousy game of golf that day, needless to say. The fact is I wasn't thinking much about my golf game. Bill and I were talking about how we were going to release a statement. Then, as we were out on the back side, Chris Duvall, who is a lawyer in our organization, came rushing out to us.

"There's a million reporters and photographers at the clubhouse." So the news had been released. I got into Chris's car and went down the back way to the locker room. In the car Chris said, "Well, son, what do you want to do?"

I said, "I don't know."

"Well, we're going to have to do something. We just can't sneak out of here."

And I said, "No, I don't want to sneak out of here. I just want to think of the proper thing to say."

In the locker room I asked for a piece of paper and I wrote

out a statement. I said that I was very sorry about my suspension, I was very sorry for what I had done, that I knew I had done wrong and that I hoped I would be forgiven and would have a chance to play again.

Chris read the statement to the reporters and then most of them left and we came out to go home. But there were still a couple of photographers around, trying to take a couple of shots of me getting into the car. Chris didn't want them to do it and I said, "Wait a minute, Chris. This is not a federal offense or anything, for heaven's sake." And the photographers took their pictures and I got into the car and went home.

Early that evening we drove to Chris Duvall's house and held another press conference. A man from the Huntley-Brinkley show had flown in from Chicago, two had come in from St. Louis, and all the local television men and sportswriters were there. We assembled in Chris's living room and I read a long statement and then they asked questions and I answered all I could and the conference lasted about an hour and a half.

Then I went home and changed my clothes. I had a date that night with a little blonde from Louisville and we went out and tried to get lost.

We didn't succeed too well. I got an unexpected phone call at the restaurant where we were having dinner. It was Bill Quinlan and he was at the airport waiting to be picked up.

You've got to know Bill to believe him. He's a tremendous guy, a big, black-haired, extroverted Irishman who is just too much. When he was in college at Michigan State he complained one day to the coach, Biggie Munn, about the Dean of Men. Finally, Quinlan said, "Look, it's either me or him." A few weeks later Bill was playing professional football in Canada.

Bill and I were very good and close friends. I had been the main speaker when they had a "Bill Quinlan Day" in his home town of Lawrence, Massachusetts. I had been there a couple of times since and I had met a lot of his friends and it's a good Irish community.

What had happened apparently was that when the people in Lawrence found out I had been suspended, they had chipped in, bought Bill a plane ticket, and said, "Go down and visit Hornung and cheer him up."

I met Bill at the airport and he was ready to take charge. "Now don't worry about a thing," he said, waving his hands in that big, imperious way of his. "I'll handle all the press conferences, I'll tell 'em. Leave everything to big daddy."

I said, "Yeah, that's all I need, Bill Quinlan directing a news conference. Instead of getting suspended, I'd get kicked out of the country. I'd end up in Siberia."

I had just been suspended and I was supposed to be in semi-hiding but naturally I had to show Bill the town. So here we were, Quinlan and me and my blonde fiancée, all over Louisville. But Quinny definitely helped me—you have to worry about him, you know, what he's going to do next —and by the time he had gone back home four days later, I felt a lot better about things.

Other things had happened in that period to make me feel better. First of all, Jantzen called back and said definitely they were going to stick by me and they came out with a statement and they were just wonderful to me and kept me in the club so to speak, and I was real happy about that.

The reaction in the press had been good, too. Mom subscribes to the Green Bay *Press Gazette*, and the day after the suspension the *Press Gazette* went around town getting people's reactions. Mostly, it was favorable. A druggist in town had pinned a crepe paper armband to his coat. At Speed's bar, one of my favorite joints in town, the trio there played only blues. At the community sing in the Lyric Lounge, they were singing sad songs—"Who's Sorry Now?" and "When Irish Eyes Are Smiling." And my teammate Fuzzy Thurston—the guy who always laughingly said, "I'm the guy who made Paul Hornung"—said, "I was thinking of retiring, but not now. He'll need my blocking when he comes back."

At first the personal reactions at home were mixed. I got a couple of long-distance calls canceling speaking engagements. My first speaking chore after the suspension was scheduled for St. Petersburg, Florida, at Notre Dame High School. They called me right away and said they didn't know whether it would be a good idea for me to come down and talk to the high school kids. Then, the next day, they called back and said they definitely wanted me there. So I went down to St. Petersburg and the banquet was a complete sellout and I was received warmly.

But the real turning point was hearing from Bob Cousy. Bob and I had become close friends three years earlier when we started working together on the Jantzen ads. They were going to have a big testimonial for Bob in Worcester, Massachusetts, in honor of his retirement from the Celtics. I had arranged, before the suspension, to be at the banquet. But now I didn't know about going. Then I got a call from Bob.

"I definitely want you at the dinner," Bob said. "I want you right there with me."

It was a tremendous affair, held in the Worcester auditorium. There must have been a couple of thousand people there including the Governor of the State. Usually at a banquet when they introduce you, you get a nice hand and that's it. But when I was introduced I got a standing ovation that must have lasted a couple of minutes.

I was all choked up and when I was able to talk I said,

"Believe me, this is a memorable night for me, a night I'll never forget. I'll never forget Bob Cousy for inviting me here and reassuring me that I'd be welcome. This is the real turning point. Now I know I can keep going. I'll do everything in my power so that the suspension will be lifted."

The Governor, Endicott Peabody, got up and said, "It is wonderful to have friends when things are going nicely. But it's even better to have them when things are going bad. He has admitted his mistakes and he wants to come back and we in Massachusetts want him to come back."

I thought that was nice of the Governor and after that dinner I felt like a million dollars.

And so started the strangest year of my life. It was strange in that I did very well financially. I traveled quite a bit for Jantzen and went to quite a few banquets. I helped a Louisville radio station in broadcasts of high school football games. I had a five-minute radio show during the football season, and a fifteen-minute Sunday night television program reading scores and commenting on the pro football games. And I worked with Bill King for Productions Unlimited. We put on a couple of rock 'n' roll shows and an automobile show, and I worked a sports show for him. The one good thing that came out of the suspension, I think, was that I found out very definitely I could make a pretty nice living on the outside without football, and that's good to know.

It was a profitable year, all right, but it was also a year I was on the sidelines in football, the first time in twenty years that I hadn't played any kind of football. And I missed that very much. I enjoy playing football. In fact, I love to play football. I would have much rather made the money that I did make in '63 playing football than I did by not playing football. I was twenty-eight years old and I felt I had a few years left and my thirst for the game was still strong and I wanted to get *every ounce* of enjoyment out of football that there was to get, while I still could. And that was one year out of my life.

So that was my sense of loss, not playing, and missing the company of the greatest bunch of guys in the world. You grow very fond of guys, you know, when you live with them for six, seven months for five or six years—you become very close. And I missed that, too.

I was in touch with Pete Rozelle a couple of times. Right after my suspension I called Pete and asked him about the Kentucky Derby. Before my sabbatical I had invited Ron Kramer and his wife, and Fuzzy Thurston and his wife, to the Derby. I didn't want to miss the Derby but I didn't want to go if Pete said no so I said, "What do you think about me going to the races, Pete?"

Pete said, "I can't tell you what to do, but as a friend I can advise you. There's really nothing wrong with it, Paul, but some columnist might see you and throw a needle into you and it could hurt you personally."

So I didn't go to the Derby. I went to Miami and watched it on television.

Another time I called Pete was when a magazine asked me to write the story of my suspension. Again Pete advised me against it. He felt it wouldn't be wise to do at that time. So I turned the magazine down. I didn't want to do anything that would put the league in a bad light, you know; or anything that would spoil my chance of reinstatement.

There may have been some people around who felt that maybe I was putting it on a little too thick, that the expressions of remorse were just an act. But it was no act, believe me. I had one objective in mind, that was getting back to football. And I knew if I was going to get back, I had to have a good record. It was as simple as that. I wasn't trying to be any hypocrite. I was just working toward one objective. I never went to the racetracks, I never went to *a* racetrack, and I love the races. I never went to Las Vegas and all the football players go to Vegas, go to the racetrack when they're in Florida and California. But I didn't want to jeopardize my position in any way.

I was sorry for what I had done, genuinely sorry, and I knew what I had to do. Hell, I still had a good time. I went out all that year and had a ball. Women weren't running away from me because of my suspension—and if they were I would have run after them.

So I wasn't out of character at all. I stopped betting and I had to be careful of my associations and all this was the same thing anyone would have done in my situation.

I visited Green Bay twice during my sabbatical. The first time was in the pre-season, a September 2 exhibition game against the New York Giants. I got interviews for my radio show from some of the boys and stayed with Max at the house and it was almost like old times. Not quite, though. At the game instead of being down on the field, I sat in the stands with Ron Kramer's wife, Nancy, and their boy. I was introduced over the loudspeaker and it was mostly all applause, though I think I detected an odd boo or two.

One of the nice things that happened to me at the game was when Mrs. Lombardi came over from her seat and said hello. "Don't worry about anything," she said, "we're going to have you back next year." Marie Lombardi is a very good woman, very close to the ballplayers. She goes to every ball game. She's one of the few women I would imagine that really understands me. Being the Coach's wife, she should. She has been very wonderful to my mother, too, and during that year I got a couple of nice letters from her and it was thoughtful of her.

That weekend I also spoke to Coach Lombardi and he

said he was real glad to see me and he said again there was a very good chance of my being reinstated.

I went back up to Green Bay once again at midseason, the week of the Chicago Bears' game. It was much the same thing. I couldn't stay for the game because I had to be back in Louisville for my Sunday show. It was just as well as things turned out. The Bears dumped us, 26–7.

With all the good things that were happening to me, I still had a feeling of apprehension, a constant apprehensive feeling. It's kind of a funny thing. Everybody kept saying it was going to be okay and that I would be reinstated in time to play next year. Still, deep down—and, mind you, I have always been a confirmed optimist—deep down was that little doubt that maybe I wouldn't be reinstated. And I had that in the back of my mind all during my sabbatical, no matter what I heard to the contrary.

Early in January I went to Los Angeles to work on Jantzen ads. I also had time to take in the Pro Bowl game. I sat with Dean Martin and at one point with the West ahead, Martin shook his head and said, "I'm blowing my bet."

I looked sideways at Martin and said, "Please don't mention that word, the bench might be wired, you know."

Another time that month I was flying to Minneapolis for an appearance and Perry Como was on the same plane. He was going to do one of his TV shows in Minneapolis. He was playing gin and I went over and watched him and he looked up and said, "Gosh, Paul, I sure would like to invite you to play, but I don't guess you need any more of this, do you?"

I guessed not, but I was cheered up when, at the annual meeting of the NFL Players' Association, they sent a resolution to the Commissioner's office asking that Alex Karras and I be reinstated.

I thought that was a fine thing for them to do, but I still

heard nothing officially from anybody in the league office. Then, around the first of March when I was in Miami, I got a call from Pete Rozelle.

"When can you come to New York?" he asked. "I'd like to talk to you."

I was thinking, oh-oh, maybe this is it, and I said, "I'll be there tomorrow."

So I put on my brightest red sports jacket (I wanted to travel incognito, you know) and I flew into New York. It was a Saturday morning and when I got to the league office Pete was there with his daughter.

What a letdown. We just talked for about forty minutes. He just went over my associations again, asked me general questions, said it had been a difficult year and he asked me my feelings on it. He asked me if I understood why the kind of thing I had done was bad and could affect the integrity of the sport. And of course I said I understood. And how I understood!

I was kind of sitting on a pincushion and after the interview seemed at an end, I couldn't hold it back any longer. I said, "Pete, am I going to get reinstated or not?"

He said, "Well, we haven't made a decision yet." Then Pete looked closely at me and my bright sports jacket and he grinned. "It might be better for you not to go into Shor's," he said, "someone might recognize you."

So I did the next best thing. I had lunch at Frank Gifford's apartment with Frank and his wife, Maxine, and Toots Shor joined us there.

And I went back to Miami that same day disappointed. I couldn't understand why I had to come all the way to New York just for a conversation. But after thinking it over, I felt that if Pete hadn't called me to New York I would have probably been a lot more worried. Now, at least, I knew something was about to happen. I could just feel it.

In Miami I was staying at the Racquet Club and Doc Greene, a Detroit newspaper columnist, was staying there, too. Doc is a good friend of Alex Karras and the next day I got a call from Alex.

Alex said, "I heard you went to New York. Tell me what he said."

And I said, "Alex, I can tell you everything he said, which wasn't much." And Alex was as puzzled as me. But a week later he got the call from the Commissioner and went into New York for the same kind of an interview.

Then, on the morning of March 16, still in Miami, I was awakened by a phone call. It was Bill King and he said only one word: "Congratulations."

You know, it was early in the morning and I'm a little punchy in the morning and hard to wake up sometimes, and I groaned, "What do you mean?"

"It just came over the wires. You've been reinstated."

Now I was wide awake, very elated, very excited, like a great big load had just fallen off my back.

The next few days were hectic. I had a million interviews and a million calls to make and everyone was calling from all over. I went right back to Louisville and took care of everything and then I called Coach Lombardi.

The first thing he said was, "We want you to come up here early and start working."

I said, "That would be a good idea. I'd like to do that."

"When do you think you can be here?"

I said, "Well, I'd like to go to the Derby, which is the first Saturday in May. How about right after the Derby?"

He sounded a little gruff over the phone. "I think it would be a good idea if you came up April 15."

So we compromised. I came up to Green Bay on April 15.

And I went up to Green Bay free in mind and very hopeful. I had a lot of making up to do, especially to the kids.

The one lesson I learned from all this business was that if anyone was hurt through the suspension—besides myself—it was the youngsters. They just couldn't understand why I wasn't playing and they weren't old enough to realize the seriousness of it.

I didn't hear so much from adults. In fact everywhere I went all year long, the people were just great to me, so nice. I would honestly say that they were 99 per cent for me, and even the 1 per cent I never ran into. And everywhere I went, the kids were so terrific. When I appeared at a store in Madison, Wisconsin for Jantzen, over five thousand kids turned out. They were hurt and upset because I wasn't playing, that's all. But I knew in my heart that I had done something wrong to them. I learned, finally, that when you are looked up to, as these kids seemed to have looked up to me, you should really try to set an example, and the better way you live your life, the better it is, naturally.

I got one letter from a mother in Wisconsin who said her boy would not watch the Green Bay Packers on television because I wasn't playing. And that touched me.

And I got letters from boys who said they remembered me in their prayers every night. "I pray for you at Mass every Sunday. . . ." "There'll be another Rosary for you this Sunday, Paul. . . ." This touches you. This was the mistake I made, letting these kids down.

And so I started back to Green Bay that April, chastened but hopeful in spirit. I felt that 1964 could really be my year of redemption. But I had to have a great year, a good year wasn't enough. I had to have a great year.

4. I CAN'T KICK

"All right," Bart Starr snapped in the huddle, "blue left, 48 option, on two."

That's my play. It starts to the left, like a sweep, and I have the option of running with the ball or passing.

We broke huddle on the St. Louis Cardinals' twenty-three with about three minutes left in the game, the Playoff Bowl they call it, between the second-place teams, in Miami's Orange Bowl. Winners get eight hundred dollars apiece, losers six hundred dollars. First and ten and we had the momentum. The Cardinals had the lead, 24–17, but we had the momentum.

"Set!" Bart shouted, looking to the left and right. "Two! Forty-one! Hut! Hut!"

I came across, right to left, running parallel to the line of scrimmage. I took the handoff and started to belly the run, to give the guards enough time to pull across behind the line to lead the play. I looked downfield, saw that Max McGee had two steps on his guy. If I threw at that moment, the ball would either have gone over Max's head or he would have had a shot at it. I wanted to be sure. I hesitated a second, and it was a mistake. Their big defensive end, Joe Robb, had broken loose from the block and he hit my arm just in the motion and I didn't get the distance on the ball. I was tackled and went down.

And when I got up and saw what had happened, saw that the ball had been intercepted, the only thing I could think of was, "The perfect ending to a lousy season."

We lost that January '65 post-season game, 24–17, and I got out of there fast because I had to be in Los Angeles to work on Jantzen sweater ads. Two days later the story broke all over the country that I was through with the Packers, that Vince Lombardi was going to get rid of me.

It made the front page of a New York newspaper. "Paul Hornung is through with the Green Bay Packers. . . . Hornung and Green Bay coach Vince Lombardi, it has been learned, reached the breaking point last week in Miami where the Packers were training for the NFL playoff bowl game with the St. Louis Cardinals." The story went on to say that I had been late for a meeting, that when I had attempted to apologize, Coach had said, "Get in your car and keep going."

Here's what actually happened.

We were supposed to check into Miami on December 26 and there was to be a meeting on the twenty-seventh. So I got in the twenty-sixth and I went over to check in at the Racquet Club, where I usually stay when I go down to Miami. We all went out that night and nobody knew exactly what time the meeting was the next day and I don't know where I got it in my head that there would be a meeting right after the championship game—the Baltimore Colts and Cleveland Browns—about six or six-thirty in the evening.

So instead of going back to the hotel that night of the twenty-sixth, I stayed at a friend's apartment. I woke up about ten the next morning and I just took my time. So at about one I'm strolling in the Racquet Club and I get a call and it's Max. "You know," he says, "you're in a little hot water."

"Why?"

He said, "You missed the meeting." I couldn't believe it. Max said, "The old man's a little perturbed. You better go see him."

I went right back on to the hotel and called him and I told him I didn't know there was a meeting scheduled and I thought there would be one after the championship game. He said, "Well, I'll talk to you tomorrow."

So we talked the next day and he was real perturbed. He said, "You should have known, there's no way you shouldn't have known." And since I was the only one who missed the meeting, I would have to say that he was right. So there was a general father-and-son chew out.

But he didn't fine me and the next few days everything was fine, everything was back on even keel and forgotten about.

At least I thought that was the case until I picked up the papers in California that said I was going to be traded. A newspaperman got hold of me out there and I said well, naturally, I'd like to play with Green Bay. I'm accustomed to Green Bay right now, but if Coach Lombardi sees fit to trade me, I think he'll do it in the best interests of the club and the best interests to myself and that's the only way you can look at anything like that. It wouldn't be tough on me, being single. I don't own a home in Green Bay; it wouldn't present any great big serious problems if I did get traded other than the fact that I want to play with Green Bay. But if it happens, I'm not going to cry either way.

So it was mostly a misunderstanding down in Miami and when I got back to Louisville Mom said, "Coach Lombardi is dying to get hold of you."

I called him. He said, "I just wanted to tell you my sentiments. I don't know where the stories started but you're definitely not on the trading block. You had a rough year and I think everything will be all right next year." So after hearing that I said, maybe I am traded. Because that's what they do. They want to talk to you first.

But Coach Lombardi has always been honest with me. He knows his players inside out. He understands me thoroughly and there's no way I can lie to him. He knows that I'm single, and he knows that I like girls, and he knows that I like a good time. And he doesn't see anything wrong with that as long as it doesn't interfere, mentally or physically, with my football.

During the training season he used to get on me quite a bit because I always came back a little heavy, and it was three or four weeks before I got in real shape. He'd say, "You're running with St. Norbert's on your back" (that's the name of the college where we train). He'd say, "You're carrying a piano." . . . You've got to do this, you've got to do that. . . . You know, when I missed a block or something. But he knew he could say that to me. I'm the kind of ballplayer, the kind of a guy that could take this. Whereas other ballplayers, if you say a lot of these things to them, might take it too seriously and it might affect them, and you have to know how to coach each individual player.

Ron Kramer, for example, will play much better ball if you don't get on his back. Ron told me that when he was at Michigan there never was a coach that raised his voice. Think about it! And then to come under a fiery kind of guy like Lombardi, it's a little bit different. But Coach knew how to handle him. I'm not saying if Ron made a mistake he never heard about it, because he did, but in a different way. In other words, Coach would really get on me for making a mistake because he knew I could take it in a coaching manner. I've always been the kind of guy who took fiery coaches well because I've had them all my life.

And Coach has never chewed me out as much as people think. In that New York story it said, "In the past Hornung has had several personality clashes with Lombardi." Well, there was never any personality clash. That's the most ridiculous thing in the world. I've never had a disagreeable moment with him. We've been together for five years, and naturally there've been a few things I've done that he hasn't quite liked. Once at St. Norbert's Max and I went out the window after curfew and he caught us. And fined us five hundred dollars apiece.

"What do you want to be, Hornung," he growled then, "a playboy or a football player?"

"A playboy!" I said. I was a little peeved at getting fined five hundred dollars, you know.

But he's fined me only four or five times, and only that one time for going out after hours. 'Course, I got a stiff fine in 1964, which added to the miseries of the year, and the circumstances were unbelievable.

It was the night before the Chicago Bears' game in Chicago and I had a date for dinner, Pat West, a real pretty girl whom I like very much. We were supposed to meet Ron Kramer and Nancy, and Pat Martin and Mary Ellen. We made reservations at the Red Carpet, which is one of the best restaurants in Chicago.

We walked in about seven. Nobody was at the bar at all, we were very early. And I said, "Do you want to sit over here?" I pointed to the lounge. "Let's sit over here," I said.

Pat said, "Oh, let's sit at the bar."

Well, I immediately remembered Rule 201, Article 5: Any Green Bay Packer caught standing at a bar will be taken care of in a diplomatic manner.

That rule was going through my mind. I had tried extra

hard all year long to abide by the rules, but I didn't want to say no to Pat. So we sat at the bar and we ordered drinks. I took one sip out of my martini and said to Pat, "Honey, it would be real unique, in fact it would be terrible if Coach Lombardi walked in here."

And she laughed. "Chicago's a big city, Paul. Don't worry about it."

She was facing the door and suddenly she turned white. "Oh, my God," she said, "there's Lombardi."

I said, "You're putting me on." I turned around and there he was, as usual, larger than life. Pat put on her prettiest smile and said hello to him. I figured I'm not going to sit here and hide. So we had a few words.

His few words were, "That'll cost you five hundred dollars."

I figured I better leave. So we went out and I talked to the headwaiter, who was scratching his head, mystified by the turn of events. "M'sieu Hornung," he said in that big-city headwaiter accent, "I knew the coach was having dinner here tonight and so I thought you were meeting him."

I said, "Well, it's just my luck. Only thing about it, I'm glad he's got as good taste as I've got in restaurants. He picked the same restaurant that I picked in Chicago and there's only nine thousand of them."

Later he cut my fine to three hundred dollars but that's the kind of thing that happened to me all during 1964. I had wanted so much to have a good year. Not a good year—a *great* year. I had thought about having a great year more than I ever had in my life. I had a lot more time to think about it, you know, sitting out my suspension. And I was snaked at every turn. My kicking became atrocious. I hurt myself. I got into a little trouble. It was unbelievable.

Yet it started off real well. Because of that year's sabbatical I knew I needed extra time to get into shape. So I reported to Green Bay in mid-April, and settled into a routine. I'd go to the stadium in the morning and Red Cochran, the backfield coach, a real great guy, would be there. I'd run twenty-four laps, which is the equivalent of a mile, trotting up and back and up and back the field. Three or four times a session I'd run up the Green Bay stadium steps—all sixty of 'em—and that helped. Then we'd do some exercises, about fifteen or twenty minutes. And Boyd Dowler or Fuzzy or one of the other guys used to work out with me. I'd throw passes to Dowler, Starr would throw passes to me.

Boyd was especially helpful. You know, he's pretty fast. And running with him helped get my legs in shape. After a couple of weeks we started striding together, hundred-yard dashes and stuff like that. It helped me just trying to keep up with him. When he's going at three-quarters speed, he's flying pretty good.

I'd work like that three days a week. Coach thought four days might be a little too much. And in the afternoons I'd play golf with the fellas, sometimes with Coach. One afternoon I was supposed to play with Coach and some of the boys and I were about five minutes late and they started off without me. I caught up with them and said to Lombardi, "Well, that's a fine thing. You could wait one whole year for me but not five minutes." He grinned.

And then it was July and we were at St. Norbert's, in West De Pere, Wisconsin, and it felt real good being a part of the team again. I was unpacking in my room at Sensenbrenner Hall when my roomie, Max McGee, came in and we shook hands. Max quickly disengaged his hand. "I don't know if I should be rooming with you," he said. "I'm not allowed to associate with gamblers."

I got a lot of that. One afternoon I was playing cribbage with Henry Jordan and he looked around and said, "I know I don't stand a chance against this big-time gambler."

Even the rookies got on me. They have to sing for their supper, you know, and one night five of them stood on chairs and sang and the lyrics went this way:

> *We know a man, his name is Paul,*
> *Won't find him in a gamblin' hall.*

The Deacon—linebacker Dan Currie—got on me pretty good, too. He caught me combing my hair in front of the dressing room mirror one morning and said, "Hey, Goldi-locks. You haven't lost much hair lately. You still look pretty good for an old man of twenty-nine."

I kept on combing and said casually, "I know one thing. I may not be the best-looking guy on this team. But I'm sure in the top *two.*"

I could see that the boys were glad to have me back, and that made me feel good. Fact is, I might have started press-ing subconsciously then. I remember Jackie Nitschke, Ray's wife, saying, "Paul's back, nothing to worry about now." Well, we had lost a championship to the Chicago Bears in 1963 and it wasn't the one man that made the difference. I could have played in '63 and we still would have lost. Hell, the team only lost two games that year. But hearing all this, I felt I had to be at my best.

The first time I carried the ball before a big crowd was in our intrasquad game in Green Bay. I went around right end for twenty-two yards and got a big hand. It made me feel real good.

The first couple of exhibition games I didn't do much. Then we played the Bears in Milwaukee and that's the day I really felt I was back home, the day I felt I was ready and really gave a boost to my confidence. I scored all twenty-one Packer points that night.

I admit I was a little nervous before the game. I wasn't

too sure how I would be received. Coach was a little worried too and he said, "Listen, if anybody starts hollering from the stands, you just let me worry about it, you just be very, very quiet, just don't pay it any attention."

There were forty-one thousand fans there, my first appearance in the state of Wisconsin since my suspension, and I didn't hear one Bronx cheer. I scored the first touchdown on an eighteen-yard pass from Bart. I scored the second one on a twenty-one yard run. I scored the third one on a three-yard run. I picked up fifty-eight yards altogether and we beat the Bears 21–7. But that was an exhibition game, remember. I thought to myself afterward, They're the champions. It's going to be a lot different against those guys September 13.

Going into that Bear game, the first league game of the season, I felt better physically and mentally than I had in any other year. For one thing, I found out I wasn't having problems with my weight that I've always had in the past. It was like I was going through a change of life or something. In years before if I didn't watch what I ate, I'd go like from 218 to 225. This year I could eat anything and I was always 215, 216. And I just wasn't hungry.

We wanted that game badly. In 1963 the two games we lost were both to the Bears. Lombardi's basic plan for the Bears was block and tackle—do it just a little bit better than the other guy.

We did have a game plan, as we do in every ball game. We found out that Roosevelt Taylor, their off-safety, was the key to their defense. In other words, if he's the safety lined up on the left side, we'd run a sweep around right. He can come all the way from off-safety and make a tackle on the line of scrimmage, he's so quick. So our plan was to keep Taylor occupied, and pass the ball to certain key men we thought were a little weaker than their other key men.

Mom was in the stands for the game and she told me afterward she was never more nervous in her life. A lot of people thought I looked nervous, that I wasn't myself. But I wasn't, really. I was really happy that the day had finally arrived that I would be back in action. I had looked forward to it for a long time.

You know, I never get excited about anything, but maybe this day was an exception.

I went out to kick off to the Bears and I had a deep feeling of satisfaction. I was back there standing to kick off, and instances, moments, flashed back, remembering the year lost, the year away from football. And I realized, this is what I want to do.

It was sunny and cool, a good day for football. Before the game I had told our offensive tackle, Norm Masters, "Be sure to hit Atkins good on forty-eight. I'll run between his legs." Doug Atkins is a six-foot-eight end, one of the great defensive ends in pro football. On our first offensive play, Jimmy Taylor carried into the line and I helped Masters block Atkins, and Jimmy went for eight yards.

We scored two touchdowns in the first half. Bart hit Max McGee for one and Tom Moore for the other. Then with fourteen seconds to go in the half, Willie Wood took a punt on our forty-eight and called for a fair catch.

Jerry Kramer rushed over to Coach on the sidelines. He said, "We're going to have a free kick." And then it snapped in all our minds and Coach said, "Yeah, go in there and ask for a free kick." The rule says that you can make a free kick after a fair catch rather than putting the ball into play from scrimmage.

So with eight seconds left I went in to try and kick a fifty-two-yard field goal.

My previous high had been a fifty-one-yarder, against the Bears in '61. This one was so different. The officials had trouble with the Bear players getting them to line up at least ten yards away from the ball. And I felt the pressure. It's different kicking a field goal when you know eleven guys are going to blow in on you. Baby, I said to myself, you got no excuses now.

Bart held and I went to it. I didn't get a good piece of the ball. It was too low and my timing was a little off. But the ball sailed straight down the middle and over the crossbars. And we left the field at halftime leading 17–3.

I kicked another field goal in the third quarter, twenty-nine yards. And in the fourth quarter I got off a forty-yard run to set up a third field goal.

This was on our power sweep, 49 right. Fuzzy and Jerry Kramer were out in front of me. I started wide and then cut back sharply outside right tackle. I beat the linebacker and then gave defensive back Dave Whitsell a hip fake and cut back hard to my left. Whitsell hit my leg but I drove through him.

Then I saw Roosevelt Taylor coming across. He was a yard in back of me and about three yards laterally away from me and I had thirty yards to go, but he's so damn quick it's unbelievable. I knew I couldn't outrun him. I tried to straight-arm him, but he came under it and nailed me. Shortly after, I kicked my third field goal, this one by twenty yards.

All in all I scored eleven points, which was the margin of difference in our 23–12 victory. I rushed fifteen times for seventy-seven yards, passed twice and completed one for nine yards, and lost seven pounds.

It was a real soothing game, "just about my most satisfying victory," I told writers afterwards. Winning the game was the most important thing but naturally I wanted to have a good day coming back.

I sat at my locker a long time. I was pooped. I needed that

game. Coach was real happy and he yelled in the dressing room, "Mr. Hornung's quite an athlete." That was something coming from him, with thirteen games still to go.

Then the next week we played Baltimore and we lost by one point, 21–20, and the margin of defeat for us was the extra point I missed.

I don't know what happened on that point. I just didn't hit it right. Usually with extra points if you get them up in the air, they're gone, and I just kicked it and it went wide by a foot. It's like those real easy golf shots you've made all your life, and then you miss one. I had hit ninety-nine consecutive points after touchdowns going to that one, so it felt doubly bad blowing it.

But otherwise I had a good game. I gained forty-nine yards in ten carries and scored fourteen points.

We beat Detroit the next week, 14–10, then the Minnesota Vikings came in to Green Bay and that was another unbelievable one.

The Vikings were winning 21–20, and we drove down the field and I kicked a twenty-yard field goal. And there was a minute left and we *didn't* win the game, 23–21. One minute to go and they had to get three points on the scoreboard. I'll take a two-point lead with a minute to go any time; let's see if the other team can win. I'd love to be in that position.

They got the ball and we kept throwing them for losses until it was a fourth and twenty-two situation from their thirty-six. So there's forty-five seconds left and you figure, fourth and twenty-two, you've got the game wrapped up. Boom—they make the first down! Fran Tarkenton, who is a scrambling quarterback, got away from three or four defenders and hit Gordie Smith with a forty-two-yard pass. And Fred Cox kicked the field goal with eighteen seconds remaining.

The margin of victory was the extra point that was blocked on me. But that's the way my luck has been. I kicked it through and it just so happened that if I had kicked it at the same height, only two feet to the left, it would have been good. But I kicked it to the right and there was one guy who had his hand up and that's the guy who blocked it.

I had a good running game against the Vikings, sixty yards on twelve carries, but that's the game I reinjured my neck. It was just like a twinge when I was tackled and it didn't bother me much that week. But the next week we played the San Francisco 49ers (and won) and I got hit early in the back of the head. There was quite a bit of pain and numbness in my arm and shoulder and I didn't play much that game.

So they fitted me out with a horsecollar, which is supposed to be strictly protective—protect me from getting my head jammed one way or another—but it's cumbersome. I'd rather not wear it if I don't have to.

But I had to. We had a key game coming up in Baltimore against the Colts. They had only lost one game and we had already lost two and if we couldn't beat them we would probably be out of it altogether.

The only light note that week came in practice one morning when Coach told us, "This is the first time in four years we're underdogs."

I walked up to him and said, "Coach, don't quote any odds, please."

I would say that game was the low point of my professional career. We lost to them, 24–21. We should have won. We had them 21–17 late in the fourth quarter when I tried a field goal that was blocked and run back to set up their winning touchdown. I missed five field goals. I had never before missed five field goals in a row in my life. I went back to the dressing room feeling depressed and Coach Lombardi called me right into his office.

He said, "I still have all the confidence in the world in you." I just stood there, still stunned, and he continued, "You've got to come out of it. You've just got to work a little bit harder at it, stay with it, and don't get your dobber down."

But I never really snapped out of it. I had that good day in Detroit when I kicked three out of four field goals, but that was also the week I hurt my neck again. The next week I missed four field goals against the 49ers and we were upset. The neck bothered me all the rest of the season and I'd play one or two series and someone else would come in, and I've always had to play the whole damn ball game to be at peak effectiveness.

Naturally, my teammates were great to me through it all. They never let up with the needle. "Well, what do you know," Fuzzy Thurston would say, "Hornung set a record today—four out of four extra points."

On the way to one of our late-season games, Jesse Whittenton was sitting with me and he said, "Well, you kicked us into second place, what are you going to do now?"

And I'd kid him right back about his play in the defensive secondary. "You made *eight* left ends All-Pro this year, you know," I'd say. I'm the type of personality who enjoys this kind of give and take. It's just like Ron said, "I'll kid you about your kicking and everything, but if any sonofagun on the outside ever kids you about it seriously, just let me kill him."

Beyond the kidding of course was the reality of a mixed-up season. We finished in second place, tied for second in fact, which I didn't like at all. When you're winning, a lot of things come easier, and every person around you is a lot more at ease. The ballplayers themselves are a hell of a lot easier to talk with and kid with. You have fun when you're winning, and I like to have fun, you know.

But I just wasn't helpful to my team. I ran pretty well when I played—415 yards in 103 carries, for a 4.5 average —but I wanted to do much better. The biggest kick I can get out of football is taking the ball into the end zone, and I didn't do that too many times in 1964. And I only kicked 35 per cent of my field goals whereas I had always kicked 61 per cent. And I definitely didn't like that.

In my speaking engagements after the season, I tried to make light of what happened. I usually started off by saying, "A man came up to me in the street the other day and said, 'How's tricks?' And I said, 'I can't kick.'"

Or . . . "I was in the locker room after the Baltimore game in which I missed five field goals. Somebody handed me a revolver and I went in the john and put it to my head and Max ran in and said, 'Paul, Paul, don't shoot, for heaven's sake!' Then Jimmy Taylor, who was standing nearby, said, 'Oh, don't worry about it—he'll miss.'"

I can be very blasé about things in one way, and yet be very different in another. I missed a field goal, I thought about it. I'd read one sarcastic letter from a fan, one out of maybe a hundred favorable ones. And the letter writer would say, "Why don't you quit," or something like that and I couldn't help but think about it. Naturally, you don't like to receive a letter like that. But if you let it worry you, then you'd be in grave trouble, you know. You have enough problems with yourself, with what *you* think about, because it's happening to *you*. And if you let it worry you about how other people think, then you're in trouble.

But for every uncomplimentary letter I received, I got many, many real nice ones. At Christmastime, 1964, I got this card from a resident Wisconsin poet and football fan:

Paul, close the door to '64
But come alive in '65.
You're still the guy to lead the Pack
Whenever you get your confidence back.
Don't be afraid what your opponents
might say
You're the best football player in the USA
Next year your rivals will see a storm
To find Paul Hornung in perfect form.

I can't say I wasn't thinking about that in the off-season of 1965. I was thinking about nearing the end of my football career, and wondering—and hoping—that I could have at least one more good year.

And there was the thought, too, when I met Joe Namath in Miami, just after he signed a reported four-hundred-thousand-dollar contract with the New York Jets—there was just that little thought:

Wouldn't it be nice to be starting all over again.

Part II

1. WEST END STORY

The city of Louisville, my old Kentucky home, sits on the bank of the Ohio River in the extreme north-central part of the state. It is the biggest town in Kentucky in every way. It is a town that manufactures many things, including bourbon. It is a town where they run the biggest horse race in the country once a year. It is an action town, and it is a town where I'd just as soon settle down for the rest of my life—provided I can escape once in a while to Miami and New York and L.A., and the other spiritual oases of this country.

Louisville has spread out quite a bit since I was a boy. Then, it was divided pretty much into two sections—the East End and the West End. I lived in the West End, in the Portland district, named after Portland Avenue that kind of bisects the section.

Portland was made up mostly of Irish people—Portland Irish they called the district. I would say it was a little below middle-income bracket—mostly ironworkers and steelworkers and union people down there.

The West End of Louisville in my day, and even before, was where most of your good athletes came from. Pee Wee Reese, the Dodgers' great shortstop, came from the West End. So did Bernie Crimmins, a Notre Dame football hero. I'm glad I was reared in that environment because I figure

it taught me a lot in those days. It was a tough neighborhood. I don't mean we had gangs like the gangs you hear
about today—the *West Side Story* kind. We had little neighborhood groups, but I never belonged to any gangs or
anything.

And when we got into fights, it was nothing real serious,
no chains, switchblades, or anything like that. It was mostly
with your fists. I'm not saying I won every fight I got into
when I was a kid, but I didn't lose all of them, either. I
learned my lesson early. One day when I was very young
I got caught in the middle of a street brawl. I got clipped
a few times from the rear and came home with a semi-black
eye. My mother took one look at me and finished the job.
She kept saying to me, "Now, Paul, you've got to learn to
defend yourself."

So I learned to defend myself.

Although I came from an Irish neighborhood, I am only
part-Irish. My father was half-German, half-Irish. My
mother, who was a Williams, was Scotch on her father's side
and Irish on her mother's side. But I guess that's enough
Irish in me to qualify for the neighborhood.

My grandfather on my mother's side came originally from
Ohio and my grandmother was born in Louisville. And they
were in the grocery business and my grandmother stayed
in the business after my grandfather died (which was before I was born). My father's family was from Louisville
and were comfortably off. My father was in the insurance
business and he and Mom had been married almost five
years before I came along. Two and a half years before I
was born he was transferred to New York and they lived in
an apartment in Jackson Heights, which is in the Queens
section of New York City. Then my mother got pregnant
and in her eighth month she came back alone to Louisville.
Her mother was home and she had her own doctor and

she thought it would be kind of nice if her first child was Kentucky-born.

So she moved over my grandmother's grocery store on 523 North Seventeenth Street. It was a white frame house with a brick front where the store was, and she shared the three-bedroom apartment with her mother and an uncle.

My mother said she had planned for a girl because she had a name all picked out, Mary Ann. If it was going to be a boy it was all settled—it was going to be named Paul, after my father.

I was born two days before Christmas, at five minutes past seven on the morning of Monday, December 23, 1935, at St. Anthony's Hospital. No fireworks, no celebrations. I just came in a snowstorm (the snow was so bad that night that my grandmother had to sleep on a cot in the hospital), came into the world weighing a little over seven pounds, but stretching pretty good, something like twenty-three inches long.

Those early years of my life, the things I'm setting down here, are mostly the things my mother has remembered and told me. My own recollections are not that strong, naturally. But I do remember that I was very fat and healthy and bow-legged as a child.

The trouble was I weighed thirty-eight pounds by the time I was a year old. So Mom took me to our doctor and she said to him, "Doctor, I'm tired of hearing people say, 'What a beautiful child, but isn't it a shame he's bow-legged.'"

And the doctor said, "Well, the only thing we can do is just break his legs."

And Mom just bundled me up and said, "Never mind," and that was the end of it. Soon after, my legs began to straighten out okay.

I loved to eat then, just as I do today. I had a big frame and it seemed I was always hungry. I'd eat everything my mother gave me except for liver, which I detested. I remember when she'd come home in the evening and light the gas stove, I'd go right over and jump up and down. I thought I was getting dinner right away.

One Sunday, when my father was still living with us, we went into Shawnee Park, which is an amusement park in town. We were all having ice cream cones, and my father had eaten his and I was finishing mine and now I wanted Mom's. And she said, "Paul, you had an ice cream cone."

I said, "Well, I want two of them."

She said, "Well, you're not going to get this one. You had one." So, very politely, I threw down my ice cream cone. And with kids playing ball around me, and nice little girls all dressed up walking by, I very politely stretched out on the pavement and kicked up a tantrum.

My mother said to my father, "Let's just leave him here."

My father said, "That's good enough for me." So they both proceeded to walk over to the car and I kind of held my head up to see where they were going, screaming all the time, and they kept walking and got to the car and stayed there. And I just saw it wasn't doing any good, so I picked myself up and went over to the car.

That was one of the few instances I remember of the family being together. When I was four my mother and father separated. After I was born my father lost his job in New York, and he came back to Louisville, and he stayed with my mother for a while but he couldn't find another job. He had a drinking problem and he was unable to overcome it and that was the end of it. He took the car and Mom kept the furniture and she went out to find a job.

Remember, it was 1939, still in the Depression. Mom got a job with the WPA (Works Progress Administration) as a clerk-typist and she started out earning about twelve hundred dollars a year, which wasn't much, but we got by.

And it never really bothered me that I didn't have a father. As long as I had baseball, football, basketball; as long as I had a mother who seemed to have everything under control, my life was sufficiently filled. We never wanted for anything. I'd often ask her, "Mom, we got enough money?" She always said yes, even those times she had spent her last quarter and wondered just how we were going to make it to the next paycheck.

Naturally, when you're a little boy, growing up, you think you've got everything in the world. I never realized our financial condition was precarious, she never let me realize it. If I ever wanted, for instance, a baseball glove, well it had to be the Marty Marion glove, the fifteen-dollar glove instead of the five- or seven-dollar glove. If you were a kid who played infield and you didn't have a fifteen-dollar glove you were nowhere, you know. And that was a lot of money in those days, but I got my Marty Marion glove.

Without a father in our house, it worked this way: My grandmother gave me the loving and my mother gave me the discipline. My mother explained it all to me—we always talked very frankly to each other. She told me that normally a child has his love provided by the mother, that a child can go to the mother when the father gets stern. But my father wasn't there so my mother had to be the disciplinarian. When it came to putting me to bed and saying, "stay there," she was the one.

She always made it a point to tell me when I was a kid that we were alone, that we were together, that we only have each other and that I don't want a son hanging to my coattails and that we'll always be friends. She kind of made a point of it when I was young that we were pals, like. When you're growing up I think it's natural for a mother who has

an only son and living alone, to form too close an attach-
ment. I'm very grateful that my mother did it the way she
did.

The way she did it when I was real young was with a
hairbrush. She was a pretty good disciplinarian, you know.
In fact it got so, that when I knew I had done something
I shouldn't have, I would bring the hairbrush to Mom and
say, "Here it is." That's what she used on my backside.

The one real discipline crisis of my life came when I was
nine or ten. About ten blocks from our house was a canal
that emptied into the Ohio River. I was forbidden to go
there because it was dangerous. But I was young and since
that was one place I had to stay away from, naturally I had
to go there.

So I went swimming there one day with a good friend,
Bobby Henken. My mother somehow found out about it and
ran over and caught us there. I got a good whipping that
night and also I wasn't allowed to go to the movies for a
whole week. That was tough punishment, too, because we
had a custom of going to Wednesday night and Sunday
afternoon movies at a neighborhood theater. Mom did let
me listen to my favorite radio programs that week, Jack
Armstrong and Captain Midnight.

She never pampered me, I can tell you that. We had
coal-heated stoves in the apartment and when I got big
enough to carry the coal buckets up, naturally, that was my
chore. I'd go down and fill the buckets with coal from the
shed in the back and bring them upstairs, maybe two trips
a day. My other chore in those days was drying the dinner
dishes, which I didn't mind so much.

There were two other influences on me when I was a
child; one was my Uncle Henry, the other was the church.

My uncle has been like a father to me all my life and I
guess that's another reason why my father's absence never

really bothered me. He really isn't my uncle. His name is Henry Hofmann and he and his wife Edna were just good friends of my parents. And they became even closer when my father left us. He and Aunt Edna would come over to the house a couple of times a week and I always looked forward to those visits. I remember I'd run over to Uncle Henry and say, "Take off your coat." I knew very well if he took off his coat, that meant he was staying.

He took me everywhere. One Sunday when I was four or five he came over and said we were going to take the train to Cincinnati and go to the zoo. But when I got to the train station and heard all the noise and the rumbling sounds and the echoes and the train's spotlight coming at me, I got scared and started to cry and my uncle had to take me home. When I got home I said, "The next time I'm going on that train." And the next Sunday he came back and this time I got on that train.

I remember he gave me an Indian suit when I was around four or five. When I say I remember, I guess I can remember the pictures that we still have. It's a funny thing —he bought this Indian suit in Green Bay. His wife was from Racine, Wisconsin, and they were up there one time and they stopped in Green Bay and bought this suit for me.

I used to love to hear the stories he told. He was especially great on Father Flanagan. I had seen the movie *Boys Town*, where Spencer Tracy took the part of Father Flanagan. One scene in particular stood out. Father Flanagan goes into the jail where a boy is locked up by mistake and Father is trying to get him out. But the jailer won't let him in.

Then Father Flanagan makes some remark in this picture and the jailer looks at him and says, "If you didn't have that collar on, I'd show you a thing or two." And with that, Spencer Tracy jerks off his coat and his collar and they get into a fight. And my uncle used to go through all the motions. He'd jerk his collar around and start swinging his arms and I was maybe seven years old and I used to bring all the kids around to show them Uncle Henry playing Spencer Tracy playing Father Flanagan.

One of the biggest things I looked forward to when I was a kid was taking a trolley all by myself, going uptown to visit my uncle to eat in the Blue Boar with him. That's a cafeteria with very good food and always a lot of vegetables, and I always liked that and looked forward to it when I was a kid, going out with him. I loved to go there and pick out my own food and pile the tray up. And my uncle would look at me and say, "Now, Paul, you can have all you want, but whatever you take, you got to eat." I don't think I ever disappointed him, not one time.

It was only a year ago that my partner, Bill King, and I went into a very fancy restaurant in Louisville. I ordered a steak and I said, "Now what kind of vegetables do you have with it?"

The waiter said, "We don't have any vegetables."

I said, "Let me out of here."

The waiter said, "Where are you going?"

I said, "I'm going to the Blue Boar."

Thanks to Uncle Henry I've had a savings account since I was ten years old. I used to put in a quarter a week and raised it to a half dollar when I got older. I'd go up every week and put it in. It was a real good deal and I think if I ever have any kids, I'd do the same thing. I can remember how enthused I was about having my own savings account. When it got to a dollar I said, "I'm not going to raise it higher than a dollar. I just want to keep it at a dollar."

And even today Uncle Henry handles all my earnings. He was and remains a big influence in my life. He formed a lot of the way I think today.

The Church of course helped form me, too. My mother was and is a devoted Catholic and she has always tried to tell me to live up to the teachings of the Church. In the early days we went to St. Patrick's Church on Thirteenth and Market. I remember after Mass Mom and I would stop by a little grotto in the back and would say a special prayer.

Then, when I was a little older, I became an altar boy. I went to a summer camp for altar boys two summers. We had prayers, morning prayers and night prayers. But we had swimming, too, and baseball and a campfire at night and hikes, just like any other camp. It was two weeks in the summer and though it was the first time I had ever been away from home, I didn't mind it at all. In fact I think my mother was a little hurt when I came back the first time and said I wished I could have stayed another week or two.

I didn't mind being an altar boy but I didn't strictly care about getting up at five in the morning and walking in the cold and dark a couple of miles for 6:15 Mass. If you wanted to be an altar boy, though, you had to take your turn with that 6:15 Mass. Nobody enjoyed it.

And, believe it or not, I was anxious to start school. Once I got into school I lost some of that anxiety and looked forward to holidays more than anything else. But it was never, "I don't want to go to school today." School always came easy to me and I liked it.

One day when I was five years old and impatient to be in school, I decided to do something about it. I went into the kitchen, put some bread in a paper bag, and went down to a public school near us and got in line with the other children. The teacher recognized me but let me in, anyway. She called home and got my grandmother; my mother was running around looking for me. So Mom came and got me and I cried all the way home because they wouldn't let me stay in school.

The next year I entered St. Patrick's School, which was six or seven blocks away. I don't remember my early teachers, only that arithmetic and figures were my favorite subject. The first nun I do remember was Sister John-David. I had her in fifth grade. She was an immense woman, very strong, very deep-throated. She was very personable and very, very intelligent and I liked her and learned more that year than I ever had.

That may have been the best year of my early life. I was ten years old and the two great interests of my life had begun to form—girls and sports.

Here I was in the fifth grade and I was walking a little girl in the eighth grade home. A fifth-grade guy going with an eighth-grade girl! That was like being the hotshot in the fifth grade. Naturally, when you're ten or eleven, girls don't mean an awful lot. I didn't have my first torrid love affair until I got to the eighth grade, but it was something that year I was ten, walking an eighth-grade girl to school.

And that was the year my interest in sports began to turn into an obsession.

2. "KEEP AWAY, KEEP AWAY"

They say I played with a ball in my playpen when I was a baby. I don't remember that but I do remember when I was a little older, I used to throw a rubber ball at a big chair we had in the living room. The chair was filled with down and there was a tear in the upholstery and I'd take the ball and go back and aim for the tear and the down would fly all over the room. Beautiful. And Mom would tell me not to do it and, naturally, the next day I would do it again.

But what best sums up my interest in sports I call the case of the Schwinn bicycle.

I was ten years old and it was the first Christmas without my grandmother. She had died the previous August and I knew my mother missed her very much. Mom always tried to make a big production of Christmas but this year, because we were now all alone, she thought she would make it a little bigger than it normally was. She had saved her money all that year because she wanted to get me a new bicycle, a forty-eight-dollar Schwinn bike. She also got me a new football and a basketball and a jacket.

So Christmas morning when I came out I was dazzled by the gifts around the tree, but I wasn't as dazzled as I should have been over the bicycle. What I did, right away, was get dressed, put on my new jacket, and take the football out.

Well, I didn't get home from playing football until late that afternoon and there was Mom kind of looking at me with hurt eyes and I think I had an idea what was bothering her.

"Ma," I said, "I'm going to ride the bicycle now."

And I took it out and rode it up and down the street once, and that was it. I came back, got my new basketball, and went into a friend's yard to shoot baskets.

That was the way I was about sports then, and even before. When I was in the fourth or fifth grade, we all started becoming interested in ball, any kind—baseball, basketball, football. Most of the kids playing on the block were older so they wouldn't let us play. We'd have to find our own outlets and yards.

I started playing basketball before anything. In Kentucky, you know, basketball is the national pastime and there were quite a few hoops thrown up all over the neighborhood. So I went out and played in backyards, on concrete, wherever there was a hoop. I loved basketball. It was always my favorite sport when I was a kid; I guess mostly because I got to play it a lot more. We didn't have the facilities to play football. If you had a good football, you sure weren't going to take it out on the concrete and scar it up. And naturally you didn't want to be running around and be falling down on the concrete.

Sixth-grade basketball was my first organized sport. I remember one incident that year when we went over to play St. Augustine, a colored school in another Catholic parish. I was, I guess, the best basketball player on our team. We got beat 66–4. I scored all the four points and I felt like I guess I was king. But the colored boys were so much better it was unbelievable. They had this brother group, the Mozees. It was a big family and there always seemed to be a Mozee playing basketball in grade school. And I'd go up after school and play with them and we got to be real good friends. I'll never forget. I was in the seventh grade and playing in the eighth-grade league now and somebody stole my tennis shoes and Zeke Mozee—he was the oldest brother at that time, he was the big honcho at the school—Zeke got them back for me. He wouldn't let anybody steal them. And we've been good friends ever since. Zeke is working in Louisville and I always see him and I see his brothers every once in a while. Louisville was a Southern city then, a lot more than it is today, and maybe a lot of people thought I shouldn't have been playing with Negro kids at that time. But I didn't care. This is the way I did things, and we always got along very well.

My love of football began about the same time. It started in school. We always had a recess, a lunch recess. The nuns used to get so mad, especially in the later grades, seventh and eighth. We used to play a game called "Keep Away," using a volleyball. You'd have sides and try to keep the ball away from the other team. And whoever had the ball at the end when the bell rang, won the game. I can remember many times coming in just filthy dirty. We played on concrete and a lot of the kids got hurt, but not seriously, and a lot of the clothes were ripped and everything. It was good, clean fun and yet it was—I can even remember in those days —pretty competitive.

So all the time in those years I was out playing. If it wasn't Keep Away, it was straight tackle football. If it wasn't football, it was baseball. If it wasn't baseball, it was basketball. I'd shoot baskets until it was dark, and when the street lights came on I'd go out again if I could. In those early years, when my grandmother was still alive, I'd come home and change my clothes and then go out and play. The big

trouble Mom had after she got home from work was getting
me to come in. I never wanted to come in. I just wanted to
stay out playing until I was so tired I fell down.

I did a lot of kicking too when I was a kid. I remember
going into vacant lots by myself, placing the ball, digging
it in the ground, and kicking it. I can remember when we
lived on Bank Street, they had a churchyard nearby and
I'd go over there and kick a football, kick it over the back-
board.

After my grandmother died Mom sold the grocery store
and the other property and we moved to an apartment but
stayed there only three months. Mom didn't like it too much;
I think she still felt lonely without her mother. So one of our
old neighbors suggested we move in with a good friend of
hers, a widow. We did and stayed there over a year, but it
was kind of crowded. She didn't have an extra bedroom so
she had to set up two Army cots in the living room and we
slept on them. I thought that was great, sleeping on an Army
cot.

From there we moved to the apartment on Bank Street,
but I just didn't like it. It was too far away from my friends,
I guess. My mother sensed this, I'm sure, because one night
at dinner she said, "You don't like it here, do you?"

"No, I don't."

"Well, I guess I'm going to have to consult you now on
things. You're old enough to know what you want." I was
fourteen and we moved again, this time back to Portland
Avenue. Two widows owned the house and they had an
apartment upstairs and we settled down and stayed there
until my senior year at Notre Dame. Then we had to move
again because Mom said there was no place to put all the
clothes I was accumulating.

I liked that apartment the best. It was right across the
street from a Marine hospital and they had terrific grounds,

and let us play ball on their property. It was very convenient and I was out there all the time.

The first organized football team I played on was in the eighth grade at St. Patrick's, and we were part of a new church league in Louisville. I remember telling Mom a year earlier how much I hoped to make that eighth-grade team. The next fall I tried out for the team and was pretty sure I'd make it, but that time there was some embarrassment over money.

We had to buy our own helmets and shoulder pads, so I came home one night and said to Mom, "Do we have enough money?"

She didn't say no; she never said no. She said, "What do you want it for?" I told her what I needed and she said, "Do you think you'll make the team?"

"Sure I will."

She said, "Well, I wonder how much it will cost?"

"I don't think it's going to cost much, but I'll find out tomorrow." It came to about eight dollars altogether and I told Mom the next day and she said, "Wait until Saturday and then I'll get it for you."

So Mom went to the store and bought the equipment, only she got the wrong color for the helmet. She got red and white and our colors were green and gold. "Mom, you got the wrong colors," I said. So we went back and exchanged it and I was pretty happy.

I made the team all right. I remember Danny Bain was the coach and I played quarterback. And this was much better than playing tackle in the streets. I was small then but I wanted very much to learn. Also, I could throw the ball better than anyone else my age. We played the split-T formation and that was fine because it was easy to learn and it meant a lot of running for the quarterback, running on option and things.

So those were good years. Father William O'Hare was the head of St. Patrick's and he was a fine man. He organized the sixth-grade basketball team and the football team and used to load us in his car and take us to practice every day after school and in the evenings.

I liked baseball too and played a lot of it in those years. In the summer if someone was around we played baseball every day. I was a catcher in grade school and when I was in the eighth grade going to St. Cecilia Parish, I made the St. Cecilia team as a second baseman. It was an eighteen-year-old-and-under team and I think I was fourteen, and a substitute infielder. Mom used to kid me that I'd come home every Sunday and she would look at me and say, "Well, I wish your uniform would get dirty." But I got to play every once in a while. The regular second baseman had to work every other Sunday for a drugstore and that's when I got in the game.

That year we won the city Church title and went to Dayton, Ohio, for the national championship. We lost two out of the three games and I played one ball game. It rained real hard and they just had to keep playing the games because all the teams couldn't afford to stay another day. We faced one very tough pitcher and everybody else struck out, almost. I hit the ball, I know that. I think I dribbled one out in front of the catcher, but at least I got a piece of the ball.

I played high school baseball until I was a senior. That year I was involved in various basketball tournaments that carried into the baseball season, so I couldn't make baseball. I did have one good year in baseball playing for the Shawnee Post American Legion team when I was in high school. I played first and second base and hit over .500 that summer. It was a fast league and we won twenty-two games and lost four, but we lost the last one, which prevented us from going into the tournament.

I remember when I was in the eighth grade all I wanted to be was a Ralph Beard. He was playing for Kentucky at the time, which had a tremendous basketball team in those days, and I watched them play a couple of times when the team came into Louisville. Beard was a fine playmaker and shot and I thought, boy, wouldn't it be something if I could go on and do as well as Ralph Beard. (A couple of years later I was a sophomore on the varsity and Ralph Beard was working out with us because he had been implicated in the point-shaving scandal at Kentucky. I felt very bad for him. You know, he had been everything and here he was, eating his heart out and not playing.)

And so I went off to high school with all those dreams and full of hope for the future.

3. A START AT BECOMING A MAN

Early in the fall of 1949, just after I had entered Flaget High, I was standing in line at the lunchroom when I overheard two older boys talking about me.

One looked right at me and said, "Who's that kid?"

The other said, "That's Paulie Miller's boy from St. Patrick's. That's his football player."

And the one who had asked about me looked at me and snickered. I was only fourteen then and I had kind of a baby face and I guess I looked small and undernourished. And he laughed and said, "How could the coach even figure this boy can play?"

I got out of that lunchroom as fast as possible, and I began to wonder about what they had said. I was supposed to be a football player but I surely didn't look much like a football player as a freshman. I had been the honcho of St. Pat's team but we only had thirty-two kids in the graduating class and now I was in a high school that was full of good athletes and had an outstanding reputation in high school athletics. And I wondered if I really could make it or whether I was just fooling myself.

It was true that I was "Paulie Miller's boy." He had seen me play quarterback for St. Patrick's and, once after a game at Shawnee Park, he had come over and introduced himself.

"I'm Paulie Miller," he had said, "you really did a good job out there." After that, though I could have gone to any one of several high schools in Louisville, I knew I wanted to go to Flaget (pronounced Flagg-é) and play for Paulie Miller.

He had only been coaching at Flaget three or four years but already he had an excellent reputation. He had learned his football when he was at Iowa Pre-Flight during World War II. He played under Don Faurot, who founded the split-T formation, and Flaget was one of the first high schools in the country to play the split-T.

So I went out to practice for the jayvees that year pretty unsure about things. I was a cautious kid in those days. Of course, I always had that air of confidence about me. Yet when you're a freshman, just like being a freshman in college, you kind of keep your mouth shut until you find your way around.

But I did make first-string quarterback on the jayvee team. The split-T was perfect for me. I could throw pretty well and I liked to move around. The guts of the split-T is the option. It's a two-on-one situation. You run down the line of scrimmage with the halfback right with you and make the defensive end play you. If he tackles you, you throw out to your halfback. If he doesn't, you cut up in the hole and run it yourself. I did pretty well that year. We won the city jayvee title and I remember the best day I had was when I hit a friend, Kirby Stone, with a couple of touchdown passes.

Kirby Stone was one year ahead of me, he was taller than me and he played basketball, too. That first year I didn't know whether I would make the jayvee basketball team or not. I didn't have the height and the basketball coach worried about me so much that he visited Mom and asked her if my father was tall. Which he was. Kirby Stone, who

lived down the street, told me he didn't think I could make
it because I wasn't tall enough. And every night while we
were working out I'd come home and ask Ma, "Think I can
make the team?" And she'd say, "I think if you want to
enough, you will, and you don't have to pay any attention
to Kirby Stone."

After that I'd come home at night and tell Mom, "They
cut two more kids and I'm still here." And they kept cutting
and, finally, I did make the team.

The best thing, I think, about that freshman year was a
friendship I made. When I was at St. Pat's I had played
football against Christ the King Parish. At halftime this kid
came over to me. He was running at halfback for Christ the
King and his name was Sipes and he looked mad.

"Listen," he said, "you guys are playing dirty out there,
piling on and all. Why don't you knock it off."

I just laughed in his face. We went out and beat them,
21–6.

The next time I met Sherrill Sipes, we had both made the
eighth-grade All-Star basketball team and we were going to
play the Flaget freshmen. We lost the game but we got
along well together and that night Sherrill slept at my house.
I remember Mom brought a whole stack of comic books and
piled them on the bed. And we spent the night reading
comic books and talking about sports, and that was the start
of a friendship that has lasted to this day. Sherrill and I went
on to Notre Dame together, we went into the Army together, and he named his first baby Scott Paul, and I believe
he got the "Paul" from me.

That year just went by so fast and then it was the fall of
1950 and now I was out for the varsity and "Paulie Miller's
boy" was putting it on the line, and I still wasn't sure
whether I could cut it, whether those guys who had laughed
at me in the lunchroom maybe weren't right.

I don't think my confidence was bolstered any by Paulie Miller's coaching ways. He was a very tough guy, and a very strong guy. He was the type of coach that, if you made a mistake, would just lose his head completely. He would get very, very excited about the whole thing. He'd get down and take the ballplayer on one on one. He got on me once in a while and I never reacted like some of the kids, and he said later he often wondered if he got through to me because I just looked like a big dumb St. Bernard out there.

He was a leader, just like Vince Lombardi is. With Paulie Miller, there were only two ways of doing it. Either you win, or you win. You might as well be in last place as second place. He had these pep talks and he'd tell us, "I'm a hard loser. I'm a great believer in winning. I believe that you need not only desire to win, but you need burning desire to win. And when you lose you should have a little tear in your eye. It should hurt real bad to lose."

At the start of the season I was still nominally on the jay-vee team, but I suited up with the varsity. There were two quarterbacks ahead of me and I saw no action the first three games. Then we were in against Manuel High School of Louisville, which always had a good football team. It was raining hard and the field was very muddy. The first-string quarterback was Rich Keeling, a senior. He had trouble holding onto the wet ball, and they put in the other quarter-back and he had trouble holding onto the ball, too. It was really muddy out there. Then Miller came over to where I was sitting.

"Well, Hornung," he said, "all you can do is fumble, too. Get in there."

So "Paulie's boy" went out there, and I was feeling much cooler than I expected. I played the rest of the way and I didn't fumble and ran the option pretty well and we upset Manuel, 12-0. From then on I started every game.

We had a pretty good team that year. We had fellows
like J. T. Frankenberger, who went to Kentucky, then
played pro ball in Canada. And Howard Schnellenberger,
who made All-America at Kentucky. The most satisfying
game of the year for me was when we beat St. Xavier's,
which made the season. They were our big rival and we
won 13–6 and I had two options and they both worked for
touchdowns.

We won six games my sophomore year but it was even
better as a junior. We had a 7–2–1 record and a lot of the
games we won big. Whenever we had a big lead, I'd go
back in the huddle and look at the boys cross-eyed or make
faces, and Sipes, who was our halfback, always used to break
up. But it kept the fellows loose.

We beat Newport Catholic in the opener 39–0 and I had
my best passing day to date, completing seven of fourteen
for 180 yards. Another big game was against St. Xavier's.
We were two-touchdown underdogs and they had us late
in the game, 6–0. Then we marched down to about their
thirty. I came up to the line of scrimmage with the option.
Then I noticed something about their defense—one of their
holes was undermanned—and I changed the play. I did it
this way: if the play was 48, I would say, 48 minus two,
or 48 plus two. This time I called for the fake option. It was
a play we had used only two or three times a year. I ran just
like I was running the option, only I handed it off to the
flanker. It worked perfectly. We scored a touchdown and
I kicked the extra point and we won, 7–6.

My biggest game that year, my biggest ever in high
school, was against Owensboro Catholic. We won, 61–7.
Everything we did worked. I completed five passes and
four were for touchdowns. I ran for two touchdowns, one
on a twenty-nine-yard sweep, and kicked seven extra points.

All told that year I scored sixty-one points and threw nine touchdown passes and made honorable mention All-State.

Now I was a junior-grade celebrity. My name started to get in the papers and Mom worried about what all that publicity and things might do to me. So one day after I had had a very good game, I was in the living room and she came in and said, "Well, Paul, how'd you feel about your game? I know you're kind of excited about it."

I said, "Yeah."

And she said, "What happened today in school? Did you go to church this morning?"

"Yes, I sure did."

"Did you give thanks 'cause you had a very good game yesterday?"

"Yes, you know what I did, though?" I said. "I just asked the Lord not to ever let this go to my head."

I meant it and I think Mom got the message. From that time on I don't think she ever worried about this any more.

Then it was basketball time, and more fun.

We had quite a team. We had Howard Schnellenberger, Sipes, myself, and a remarkable kid named Jerry Harper, who was a senior. He was a very unique boy. As a freshman he was six feet four and had never played basketball. When they got him out for basketball, he was a sophomore on our jayvee team. He used to stay on the court at halftime and shoot while we went down. He couldn't dribble the ball from here to this wall, but he could jump, he could really jump.

And Paulie just kept working with him, telling him to keep the ball tipping it up, tipping it up—taking two steps and dropping it. And the kid really worked hard. By the time he played a little bit when he was a junior he started coming around. He knew that when he got the ball, he'd take one step with his left foot and go up and try to lay it as close to the thing as he could. That's all he knew how to do, and he couldn't shoot a jump shot, or foul shot. He'd miss every one. He couldn't do anything with finesse. But by the time he was a senior he was All-City center and All-State and he went on to Alabama and made All-America. And Harper was the main reason we won sixteen of twenty-six games that year.

And after the basketball season I went on to play baseball and that year we won the city championship and I batted over .300.

So there was never any letup. Never. During school, my schedule was bang-bang. I'd grab the bus for school at eight in the morning, and football practice started at three and lasted until five-thirty or six. Then I'd take a bus home and always have an hour or more for homework. During the basketball season it was even more hectic. Playing for the jayvees we wouldn't get the gym until five o'clock, so after school Sherrill and I would walk two miles to his home. We'd have a snack, hang around, then catch a bus. It was a forty-five-minute bus ride to the Columbia gym, which was in the middle of town. Then after practice we'd take a bus our separate ways and I might get home by seven-thirty or eight and it was a late supper every night.

By this time Sherrill and I were just about inseparable. Every week he'd spend a night at my house or I'd spend a night at his house. In the summer Sherrill and I caddied together and worked a lot together cutting grass and delivering papers. We'd also go out on double dates all the time.

The big event of my junior year, after I turned sixteen, was when my Mom bought a car. A few nights before she came in and her face was glowing and I could tell something was doing.

"I'm going to take some money out of the bank," she said, "and buy a car. But first we've got to lay some ground rules."

That was okay with me. The ground rules were that we shared the car, that I could drive it only once in a while until I was a senior. Then I could have it for dates.

It was a yellow Chevvy and Mom always said it was the cleanest car in the West End. It should have been. I was always washing it. I loved that car more than I've ever loved any car in my life.

It was Sherrill who supplied the car for dates most of my junior year. That summer, before I was a senior, we'd go to the drive-in movies, three or four couples in the car and it would get a little crowded. But it was the only way we could all go, you know.

When we weren't tooling around, we would go to one of the teen-age clubs in town, and to the YMCA on Friday night for the dance. The big nights of the week were Wednesday and Friday and you had to be a real big kick. You'd save the best clothes for those nights. Corduroy coats were real big then and I was always pretty conscious of my appearance and wanted to dress nice. I had to be in at twelve midnight then. A lot of times I would be late but I'd call and Mom would know I was making some excuse, but at least I'd call.

I never went steady or anything in high school. I never had too much of a problem getting a date without having to go steady. The closest I came was when I was a senior and a story goes with that.

I had an elective class in high school and it was the fun class of my whole senior year. It was mechanical drawing. The Brother was a very funny, jovial fellow. We just had a great class—all the football players were in there and there were always a lot of laughs. Anyway, it was getting time for the senior prom. Well, I was always kind of a nut in high school—everybody was going to the senior prom and I didn't have a date for it. There were two or three girls that I was dating, but I didn't particularly want to take them to the dance—just to take a date to it. I told them, "Well, there's no use me asking just any girl to go to the senior prom."

But John Noon and a couple of the other fellows I played ball with thought it was very bad I wasn't going to the senior prom. And they decided they were going out to some of the clubs and find somebody whom I could take to the prom.

Well, they talked me into going out one night and I thought, all right, find me somebody and I'll go to the dance. So I met this girl named Ramona about ten days before the prom and I dated her. I dated her forty straight nights after that. We just started to hit it off real well. It was kind of unique, you know, and it was a big love affair.

So after I met Ramona I'd go into class and we'd say our opening prayer—"Our Father," or something else, like you did in every class when the bell rings—and then everybody would start to sing and hum, *"Ramona, how I hear the mission bells . . ."* The song had just come out and we'd have our work and start to work on it and everybody would be singing *Ramona.* And everybody would talk about everybody's girl friend and we'd just kid each other. And we sang it every day.

So I took Ramona to the prom and we had a good time and now she's probably married and must have five kids.

By the time I was a senior I was no longer small or undernourished. I was six feet two and weighed 185—built pretty much the way I am today, no shoulders, no big, massive chest, but very strong in the thighs and legs. When Paulie Miller saw Sherrill and myself at the opening day of football practice on August 15, I got the idea he was glad to see us.

He was, as I found out a few days later.

It was in a scrimmage and I was running the option. I cut

back and felt something give in my leg. I limped back to the huddle and said, "Coach, I just heard a crack in my leg."

Paulie Miller turned green. What had happened was that playing baseball that spring I had broken a bone in my leg sliding into base. Now I was a little concerned that I might have rebroken it. Paulie was very concerned.

"Put ice on it! Put ice on it!" he said. After scrimmage he bolted over to me. He had been doing some deep thinking, I could see that. "I've got a staff meeting right now," he said. "You go in the chapel and start praying till I get out of the meeting."

I did just that and then Paulie and Ray Doyle, a local citizen and backer of Flaget, picked me up and we went to St. Elizabeth's Hospital to have the leg X-rayed. Paulie seemed kind of anxious because he said to this sister, "Can you read X-rays?"

She said, "I'm not supposed to but I can."

"Well," Paulie said, "would you please look at it and tell me what you see." She did and said it looked to her that there was some calcium loose but there was definitely no break. Paulie let out his breath then, and I felt better, too.

I was able to play the opener against Cincinnati Elder, but Paulie Miller was taking no chances. He installed the shotgun attack for that one game. That's where the quarterback stands a few feet back from the center, and doesn't have to scramble quite as much. We won the game 18–7, and I hit with two touchdown passes, one to Sherrill.

We kept on winning. We beat Hamilton of Ohio 32–0, and Sherrill had a tremendous day, scoring four touchdowns. Then we played Male of Louisville before fourteen thousand people. That was a big one. Male had won fifteen straight going into that game and I believe they were favored. But we beat them 28–12. I ran a bootleg twenty yards for one touchdown.

We murdered Manuel 48–7 and I remember one thing about that game. Once in a time-out we had the ball on our thirty and I went over to the sidelines to talk to Coach. He said, "I want you to run the option, then come back with the pass."

I was feeling pretty cocky. "Coach," I said, "if you want to run that pass play, you better run it now 'cause we'll score on the option."

"Go out and do what I told you!" he exploded. So I did. I ran the option, tossed it back to Sherrill, and daylight opened up and he went seventy yards for the touchdown.

Then we beat St. Xavier 39–12 and we were city and state champions.

There were only two disappointments that season. We went all the way to Chattanooga in a bus to play Chattanooga Central. The bus broke down and we couldn't get off and everybody got sick. We got there like twenty minutes before the game, all psyched out. The best we could do was tie them, 7–7. My big disappointment was missing a field goal from the nine; it missed by about six inches.

One of my biggest thrills that year was a game we played in Mount Sterling, Kentucky, in the Recreation Bowl. We were rated with our opponent, Lafayette, as the best in the state and, naturally, the winner would be recognized as No. 1. We won the game 39–7 and I had a good enough day to be named Most Valuable Player. But what sticks out in my mind about the game was my kicking.

I had this one ball that I used to practice with before games. It was soft and naturally you could kick it easier because it was deflated a little. I used to practice with that one and kick it deep into the end zone.

Well, I had kicked the extra points after each touchdown and they went into the stands and we had lost about four or five balls. All of a sudden, I'm running back ready to kick off and they threw a ball from our side (we had to furnish the balls) and here comes my favorite little ball. I kicked it all the way out of the end zone and into the stands. Bear Bryant, who was head coach of the University of Kentucky at the time, was there and they said he almost jumped out of the press box. Which didn't hurt my standing at U. of K.

So it was some season. Both Sherrill and I made All-State and All-Southern. That was the year Sipes set the all-time city scoring record with 139 points. I ended up with four touchdowns scored, with seventeen touchdown passes and twenty-nine extra points. And I was named No. 1 high school football player in the state of Kentucky.

And the basketball team went on and did almost as well as the football team. We had a real good team. Sherrill averaged about eighteen points a game, I averaged fifteen, the other guard averaged about ten, the other forward about fourteen, the center about sixteen. That year we won the Owensboro Invitational Tournament and then, in January 1953, we won the Louisville Invitational. And that had to be the biggest thrill I ever had in basketball.

We beat a tough team from Ashland and we had to do it in overtime. And I set a new scoring record for the tournament with thirty-one points on thirteen field goals and five out of nine free throws.

There were other good games, too. We won our first regional championship ever by beating Male, 66–54. Kenny Kuhn, a great all-around athlete, who later signed a $50,000 bonus baseball contract, got twenty points for Male, but not enough.

Another fine Louisville player that year was Charlie Tyra, who played for Atherton High and later became an All-America at the University of Louisville. We played Atherton in a close one and I was out most of the game with a bum ankle. We were losing 53–50 with something like thirty seconds left and Coach let me in. I was lucky to get two quick baskets and we beat them, 54–53.

But our biggest disappointment was in the state tournament in the Memorial Coliseum. We were rated No. 1 in the state and were favored to win, but everybody choked in our first game. There were thirteen thousand people there and I was going to have the night of my life. I hit my first two shots, then three foul shots, and with four minutes gone I had seven points. And that was the end. I never hit another shot. We got beat bad.

All in all, though, it had been a fine season. I was a unanimous All-District choice along with Charlie Tyra, and Sherrill made All-State. I ended up fourth in scoring in the city. Tyra was first, Kuhn second, Sherrill third. We finished with a 28–4 record and mostly it was a ball.

That, I would say, was the happiest period of my life. Naturally, I've gotten a lot more out of life in the last few years than I ever had in my life. But I'm talking about a time when there were just no worries and you were living for a while and only for a while. High school is the start—when you start to become a man, when you start to enjoy life, really. Like getting out a little bit and learning by experience more than anything, and always enjoying what you learn. And anybody who says they didn't enjoy their high school life I think would be lying. I had a ball in high school. Even if it was an all-boy's high school, you know.

4. THOSE FRIENDLY, FRIENDLY PERSUADERS

The college recruiters first started coming around when we were juniors. Sherrill and I had made up our minds that whatever college we decided on, we were going together. So when we started to get invites to visit campuses, I'd say, "I'm bringing Sipes with me"; or Sipes would say, "I'm bringing Hornung with me." Every school that wanted me, wanted Sipes, too, so it wasn't too difficult.

When I was a junior I could almost feel certain that I was going to get a scholarship to the University of Kentucky, Indiana, or some college in the area. Even in our junior year we'd go up for a game at Kentucky, and they'd show us around and treat us very carefully.

And then when we were seniors the offers really started coming. I think I had thirty-five firm offers, and I know a lot of other schools wrote me and were interested, but once they found out that Notre Dame was in the race, they kind of backed out. Those days, being from a Catholic family and Catholic high school, it probably seemed like Notre Dame had a lock on me. Which wasn't true at the time.

Some of the offers, naturally, were wild. I won't mention the schools but I received a couple of money offers and one was kind of fantastic. They offered me ten thousand dollars in the bank, guaranteed, when I graduated. They offered

me a new car and a scholarship not only for myself but for a
girl. They said, if you've got a girl friend, we'll give her one,
too. And they offered clothes and spending money.

That one seemed just a little much and I wasn't tempted,
but some of the others really excited me. I'm thankful to this
day that I had my mother and Uncle Henry as my advisers.
They helped keep me from floating off into space.

Some of these recruiters thought they were shrewd. They
figured the soft underbelly to Paul Hornung was through his
mother. How wrong they were! She never budged an inch.
She was like a rock. One day a college recruiter came over
to the house and said to Mom, "Mrs. Hornung, wouldn't you
like a new house?"

"I'd like a new house," Mom said, cool as a princess, "not
now, though."

They tried all kinds of things on Mom. They figured, ah,
here's an only boy's doting mother. They'd phone her or
come to the house and say, "Our school would really be better for Paul."

And Mom would say, "Well, why?"

And they'd say, "Well, because we're nationally known
and if he's going to play pro ball someday, he ought to start
here."

And she'd say, "Well, golly, that's too big a jump for me.
He's just getting out of high school, he's got to play four years
of college."

One day an assistant coach from a Southern college came
to see Mom. He was pretty direct.

"Mrs. Hornung," he said, "I understand that your boy is
not leaning toward our school. Well, we can only give
him ten more days." Mom didn't flicker an eye so he stepped
up the attack. "I know that you're a very good Catholic, Mrs.
Hornung, and that you probably talked to Paul about it, but
I'll tell you one thing about our school. One Sunday we

take all of the boys to a Catholic church and one Sunday we take them to a Protestant church. Another Sunday we take them . . ."

"Whoa there," Mom said. "I expect when they get to college, they ought to be able to go to their own church, and not make the Catholic boys go to the Protestant church, and not make the Protestant boys go to the Catholic church."

The coach got all flustered. "Well, Mrs. Hornung," he said, "I didn't really mean that."

It's lucky Mom held out the way she did because I was very susceptible. Every time Sherrill and I visited a campus I'd come back all excited and sold, dead sold on it. And I'd say, "Mom, we're going there." And Mom had to calm me down.

She'd say, "This pressure is just beginning, Paul. And when you get older, you'll understand. You're a man now. You've got to make up your own mind and have a reason for it, not because you had a good time this weekend." But that never stopped me.

Sherrill and I made quite a few trips together that spring of 1953. We visited the University of Florida, Purdue, Vanderbilt, Georgia Tech, Indiana, and Notre Dame. The trips were all great but the best one, I guess, was the University of Florida.

Only we almost didn't get there.

One day we were invited to dinner—Mom and I, Sherrill and his parents—at the house of a big U. of K. backer in Louisville. An assistant coach of Kentucky was there, too. We were about to fly to Gainesville. I was kind of leaning there at the time, just as I was kind of leaning to Vanderbilt when I was there, and Indiana when I was there. Our host knew we were going to Florida and I guess he was afraid we might sign. So he took us outside and showed us his brand-new Cadillac.

"Boys," he said, "if you don't take that trip to Florida, I'll give you this Cadillac to drive to Florida—and *I'll* pay for the trip."

Naturally, we said okay and he said, "Go ask your parents." So we went in and asked them and they both said no, and we had to say no.

So we went to Florida and when we got off the plane they drove us to Daytona Beach for a couple of days, and left us with a car and a cottage, and fixed us up with dates.

I was really amazed at the way they treated us. There was no hard pressure at all. This was one school where they were more anxious to get Sipes than me. They wanted him real bad, and Sherrill was wavering, and the way they treated us didn't hurt.

After our little siesta in Daytona, we went up to Gainesville and toured the school. One of the coaches then came over to talk to us. He said, "Well, you've seen the school, do you like it?"

I said, "I sure do, it's just beautiful."

And the coach said to me, "Well, we know you're interested in Notre Dame and we sure would like to have you down here, and we sure would like to say to the press that you decided to accept here."

I was ready for that. My speech was all made out. I said, "Well, I'm very interested but I can't sign anything. I promised I wouldn't sign anything." Then I said, "I do think in all honesty that I'm going to Notre Dame."

And the coach said, "Well, fine, we wish you all the luck. We hope you have just as good a time at Notre Dame as you would here."

And we stayed three more days and there was no more pressure—it was just beautiful.

Finally, though, I had narrowed it down to three schools —Indiana, Kentucky, and Notre Dame.

All this time, there was never any trouble about grades. We both had 'em and we could have gone anywhere we wanted. Sherrill and I were in Class 207, the top class at Flaget, and we were both honor roll students. I was always good in algebra and physics. I had a definite aptitude for engineering when I went to Notre Dame, but they kind of talked me out of that. Too many labs for a football player, they said. So I went into business administration.

At this time, I was leaning toward Kentucky and Sherrill and Mom were leaning toward Notre Dame. My big high school idol had played quarterback there, Babe Parilli. I had a lot of friends there. I wanted to stay in Kentucky and if I went there I would have been eligible to play varsity ball as a freshman. And Bear Bryant had as much as told me, "You come to Kentucky and you're our No. 1 quarterback next year." It was as simple as that.

But first I had to eliminate Indiana, and that was a little difficult.

Bernie Crimmins was head coach at Indiana then and he came from the West End in Louisville and all the Crimmins family was from the West End. Sherrill and I played ball with Steve Crimmins, Bernie's kid cousin. Another cousin, John Crimmins, got me my first legitimate job when I was a junior in high school. That summer I worked at the courthouse as a clerk.

About eight of us from Flaget went up to Indiana for one of the games. Later we went back a couple more times to visit the school. I liked Indiana. I remember one time coming back and telling Mom, "There's a chapel over there. It's not a Catholic college but there's a chapel."

I might have ended up going to Indiana but for a rumor that got out about my conduct there; that kind of soured me on the school.

It went this way:

One of the coaches had walked into Bernie Crimmins' office and there was Hornung sitting in Crimmins' chair with his feet up on the desk, saying, "If I come here, coach, you're going to have to match this and match that." First of all, when you're seventeen years old—even today—the kids don't have the guts enough to say, well, I'm getting fifty thousand dollars here, I want you to match it. This is a little bit too strong. And then I would never do it in the first place —and I never did do it. But, you know, a couple of kids in Indiana heard this and the rumor got around that Paul Hornung had his hand out.

So I eliminated Indiana, and now it was Kentucky or Notre Dame. And Kentucky worked very hard on me. And on Mom.

Bear Bryant had been down to see Mom a couple of times. And he was a charmer. Mom always said, "What a good-looking man, and is he ever a salesman!"

He came to the house the first time and Mom said, "Would you like some coffee, Coach?"

And he said, "Why, you are a doll." And he came right into the kitchen and he was so big and the kitchen was so small, and Mom couldn't put on. What did she have to put on for?

So she fixed him some coffee and said, "Let's just sit here in the kitchen and drink it."

He said, "That's fine." And he talked about the U. of K. He told Mom about the campus and asked if she had ever been there (she had). And he invited her back to stay in his house with Mrs. Bryant. And he went on to tell what he could do for me, how he could make a great player out of me. And when he saw Mom hadn't been moved at all he said, "Mrs. Hornung, I sure do appreciate the coffee, and I'm coming back to have some more."

Then he sent a man who came from one of the prominent Catholic families in Louisville. He knew my grandmother and so he felt he could talk very frankly to Mom.

He said, "Mrs. Hornung, you will have a Cadillac at your disposal during the season. You won't have to drive the Cadillac. If you're tired, you can lie down and go to sleep and we'll take you to all the games in the Cadillac."

And when Mom seemed unmoved he looked around and said, "Maybe you wouldn't have to live here."

Mom said, "We've been very happy here."

And then he looked at Mom and said, "Mrs. Hornung, I'm not impressing you a bit, am I?"

And Mom said, "Well, I don't think you're trying to. You're just telling me the plain facts." She was a jewel.

But when I heard the facts I became all excited and dazzled and I jumped on Mom and said, "What do we do? What do we do?" That was the system in those days in recruiting high school athletes and the system is the same today, only probably more so. And can the fellow being recruited help but be dazzled by it all? I don't especially think it's 100 per cent right. All that pounding on a boy, all that talking, and talking, and talking. Talking as much as they can and putting every bit of pressure on you. And if you weren't tough enough, or if you didn't have good advisers, you were lost.

I think this kind of thing spoils the high school athlete. In the first place he starts off college right away with a reward for not doing a thing. In the second place, he forgets that getting a good college education is the main goal, or should be. I would say that about 90 per cent of the college-recruited athletes don't think of this because they're just not serious enough about things academic. I remember when I was a seventeen-year-old freshman, all I wanted to do was play sports; I would much rather have been out practicing basketball during the basketball season than putting in four extra hours on trigonometry.

I don't know how the system can be bucked. I didn't buck it then and I probably wouldn't today, I'm no great reformer, you know, but I do feel that all that high-powered recruiting does things to anyone who possesses any kind of values.

But the pressures never let up.

One Wednesday around five in the afternoon, Mom had just come home from work and I was in my room napping when a car drove up. Mom recognized Bear Bryant when he got out, but she didn't immediately recognize the gentleman with him. Mom stood at the top of the stairs and said, "Is that you again?"

And Bryant laughed and he turned around to the other man and said, "See, I told you about her."

And she saw this other man glance up and say, "How are you, Mrs. Hornung?"

Mom said, "I'm all right." Then she kind of backed up because she recognized the man. And she said, "Coach, is that —is that the Governor with you?"

Bryant said, "Sure is."

"For Pete's sake. Well, come on up."

She had a little short apron on, and she had just ironed curtains and all she could think of, when she realized it was Governor Laurence Wetherby, was, "Oh, my Lord, my curtains are on the divan." And when they came up she was kind of flustered and said, "Now don't sit on my clean starched curtains."

Then she recovered and offered the Governor a soft drink. Bryant said, "She makes good coffee."

Mom said, "I do not, not good enough for the Governor." And the Governor said he didn't take coffee anyway.

She offered to wake me but Bryant said no. "No need to

call him," Bear said. "We're taking him to lunch tomorrow."
(They did, too, and I came home right away and I said to
Mom, "I want to sign with U. of K.")

Governor Wetherby was a fine-looking man, very distin-
guished, a sincere gentleman. There was no high-pressure
sales talk. He just said to Mom, "Keep the boy in Kentucky.
We can do so much more for him when he gets out of
school."

Then Bryant started talking and by this time he and Mom
were friends and she could kid with him. She said, "Don't
you try to con me—don't you try to sweet-talk me. You know,
I still have the rosary beads out for him to go to Notre
Dame."

And Bryant made believe he was astonished. "Oh, you
can't say that, Ma'am. We've got this priest who's going to
take care of Paul when he gets to Kentucky."

They must have spent forty-five minutes with Mom and
she kept her head all the time and when they were gone all
she said to me was, keep an open mind. But it was getting
harder and harder to keep that open mind. And Mom wasn't
kidding me at all. I knew she wanted me to go to Notre
Dame.

Actually, I had never thought it was such a bad idea.
When I was a kid, ten or eleven, Uncle Henry always used
to tell me that someday I'd be a Notre Dame fullback. Then
when I got older and it looked like I might be a football
player, Uncle Henry kept saying, "If you go to Notre Dame,
you not only have to be a good football player, but you
have to be a good student." Then later, playing with the best
team in high school, I wanted to see if I could play with the
best team in college. At that time Notre Dame was playing
the best football, playing the best teams in the country. And
after I got a good clear picture of the other schools, I kind of
wanted to go to Notre Dame and see if I could play there.

Notre Dame didn't come after me quite as strongly as
some of the other schools did. They never even scouted our
games. The first I knew they were interested in me was
when they wrote Coach Miller and asked him to send films
of Sherrill and me in action. (Notre Dame Athletic Director
Moose Krause said Sherrill and I were the only kids up to
that time ever offered full-time scholarships on the basis of
the films alone.) Next thing I knew we and a lot of other fellows were invited to South Bend for the Southern California
game. After the game we met Frank Leahy, the head coach.
But that's all there was to it; no commitments, no offers
were made by anyone.

A month or so later a fellow named Bill Veeneman called
home and talked to Mom. Bill and his brother Jack are both
Notre Dame grads and their father is chairman of Churchill
Downs, home of the Kentucky Derby, and they're a real
wonderful family. And of course, they're all for Notre Dame.

Veeneman said Frank Leahy had spoken to his dad and
Leahy had reviewed our films and had said, "Do you know
this boy Hornung? I think we want him. Go see Mrs. Hornung. Find out what kind of a boy he is and his background
and about his family."

Then Mom got a call from a Notre Dame recruiter in the
area, Rog Huter. This was after I had heard from Georgia
Tech and Indiana and Kentucky and pretty near everyone
else; Notre Dame was kind of getting into the act late. Huter
told Mom to hold me still, see that I didn't make any commitments yet. A few days later, Bob McBride, who was
Leahy's chief assistant, came in to see me.

McBride impressed me very much. He was a very
straightforward man. He told me that I had the grades for
Notre Dame, and that Sherrill had, too. He said first that
he didn't want to put it on a monetary basis but aside from
the religious angle, which he knew he didn't have to sell

me on, an education at Notre Dame was comparable to eight
or ten thousand dollars. He offered a four-year scholarship
—tuition, room and board, books. And if we wanted to go on
to graduate school he said we could probably become assistant coaches. But he said that we had to make the grades,
that we couldn't play unless our grades averaged at least
77 per cent. There were no gimmicks. Then he invited us
up to Notre Dame.

So we drove to Notre Dame with Rog Huter. It was now
in the early spring and it was very cold and very damp. We
didn't have overcoats and we froze to death. We stood in
the middle of the Notre Dame campus. It was stripped bare
and all the kids were in class and everything seemed gray
and desolate.

I looked at Sherrill and Sherrill looked at me and I said,
"Let's don't go here."

And Sherrill said, "Right, let's get out of here."

Then they took us to see Coach Leahy.

Here was one of the world's great salesmen. He could
have sold ice cubes to the Eskimos in winter. He was sitting
behind his desk, wearing those rumpled clothes of his, and
his lined face looked worried and concerned. Then he ad-
vanced on us and shook our hands and broke into a smile and
put his arms around us.

"Lads," he said, "you would both look awfully good in
green. And Our Lady needs you here."

The feeling we got, us simple high school kids, was like
we were talking to a saint; not a coach, not a man—something a little above.

And he kept on talking, always with that sad, saintly look
in his eyes. "Lads like you belong in a Catholic college. You
belong to Notre Dame. You should matriculate at the finest
university in the world. If you're going to play professional

football, there's a back door and there's a front door. This is the front door. You'll be nationally recognized." Then he looked right into my eyes and said, "Paul, not only will you get a good Catholic education here, but I think I can make you the greatest football player in the country."

There was silence for about ten seconds, then Sherrill said, "Where do we sign?"

Leahy smiled softly. "We don't sign anything. We just shake hands." We shook hands and if ever you have experienced a warm handshake, this was it.

We left campus that night reeling, like we had just left a corner of heaven.

"Mom," I said when I got home, "I think I'm going to sign with Notre Dame."

She started. "You're kidding!"

"I'm not kidding."

"Do you mean it?" she said. "You're not reacting to pressure?"

"No," I said, "I'm not."

On July 17, 1953, I wired Frank Leahy. I said, "I've finally made up my mind. My mother always wanted me to go to Notre Dame and I've always been inclined to go there myself."

Then Sherrill and I and Rog Huter went to the sports department of the Louisville *Courier-Journal* and gave them the story. They asked me what had made me decide on Notre Dame. I said, "I had to, or there wouldn't be a priest in Louisville that would talk to me."

I was feeling real good now, like a big load had suddenly been lifted from my shoulders.

I think the real reason I signed was because of Coach Leahy. He was so impressive, just too much. Of course, Leahy went ahead and retired after my freshman year and I felt real bad about that. I had wanted to play under him.

Looking back, I doubt now whether I would have gone to Notre Dame had I known Leahy was not going to be there.

But at the time I made my decision, I was really looking forward to Notre Dame, to beginning my college career. The only thing is, once I got to Notre Dame I was overwhelmed by just an opposite feeling. At the beginning of my freshman year I felt I had made the greatest mistake of my life.

5. BIRTH OF GOLDEN BOY

We had been at Notre Dame about two months when Sherrill and I composed a letter to the University of Miami saying we wanted to transfer there.

It wasn't any one thing that went wrong. It was a collection of things, and we wanted out.

It started, I guess, the first time I set foot on Notre Dame's practice field. There were only about *thirteen* freshman quarterbacks trying out and I got to throw maybe ten passes that day.

There were some good ones, too. There was Jack Witucki, whose father Bernie was an assistant coach at Notre Dame. Jack was a high school All-America quarterback from Tulsa, Oklahoma. He and I were supposed to have been the biggest quarterback honchos in high school in our senior year. He threw the ball real well and I could see right then that he would be my main competition.

Then there was Dean Studer, whom they later switched to halfback, and Larry Cooke, and John McDonnell and Pat Flood. Pat was a very, very brilliant boy and he was on a Navy scholarship. He took the Navy test after his freshman year and scored highest in the country, and so he went on to the Naval Academy. He wound up playing behind George Welsh, Navy's All-America quarterback.

Anyway, they all looked like good quarterbacks to me. They all had strong arms. My main weakness then was passing. I could throw the ball a long way, but I wasn't too accurate a short passer—I never had been. I just didn't have that much practice in high school since we never averaged more than fifteen passes a game. So I had to work on that.

Also, I had never played defense in high school and these were the years when you had to go two ways in college. I had to learn something about defensive football. But this didn't bother me too much because I was big and I always liked the contact.

The main thing in my favor then, I think, was that we had played a split-T in high school and we played the split-T at Notre Dame. So much of the fundamentals were the same. As I said, Paulie Miller was such a great fundamental offensive coach as far as I was concerned, there wasn't too much difference between high school and college. The holes might have been numbered differently but the maneuvers were the same.

Terry Brennan was our freshman coach and I liked him very, very much; and Frank Leahy was always around. He came over to talk to us that first day. He was as persuasive and eloquent as ever. He said, "Prepare yourselves, lads, for the great days ahead as you matriculate at Notre Dame . . ." He was especially nice to me. I don't know if you would call it preferential treatment but he'd always want me to come out early to kick with Johnny Lujack. Johnny was quarterback coach then and I'd get out there and punt and kick early. Then, like on the Thursday before the game, the varsity would run back kickoffs and kickoff returns and go over that, and Leahy would bring me up from the freshman team to kick off to the veterans.

I think it was Leahy more than anyone who actually kept me at Notre Dame because I remember that we were very,

very disheartened, Sipes and I. We never played any games as freshmen, we were just part of the hamburger squad. We scrimmaged the varsity and they made hamburger out of us. We got the hell kicked out of us every day.

I can remember the first scrimmage I had against the varsity. I had a real good day. Southern Methodist, the year before, had come out with this "Benners" thing. Fred Benners was a lean, lanky quarterback for S.M.U. and to give him better protection they had put in a spread formation, something like the shotgun, with Benners riding back deep in the pocket. It had given Notre Dame trouble that year and they were worried about it for the upcoming S.M.U. game. So they had me in the spread and we practiced in the stadium—freshmen against the varsity—and I completed three or four passes and I ran the ball out of the pocket a lot of times and we went down the field a couple of times on them.

Then Leahy came over and talked to the freshmen as a group. He said, "What a great job you're doing, lads," and this and that. Naturally, now, after being under so many coaches, I can imagine what he told the varsity when he went back and talked to them alone. I can just imagine hearing him down there:

"You let that Hornung run around the end! If he does it again . . . if he's not carried off the field . . . if you don't hit him!" You know, forget about it. So they got me in the second half. On the first play I ran out of the pocket and ran an end run and they carried me off with a leg injury.

That was bad enough but we were having troubles with our grades, too. I had a couple of subjects where I was on the borderline—at the seventy-seventh percentile. One was accounting, which I hated in college, anyway—not that it was difficult or anything, but it was time-consuming. The homework every night would be an hour and a half. They worked us on the field for about two hours and forty-five minutes and after dinner I felt like going to sleep, I was so tired. And that was how I fell behind in accounting.

And Air Force Reserve was always a tough class, too. If you didn't keep up on it assignment after assignment, you fell behind. And the exams were tough. So we had to have a couple hours of tutoring for each subject.

Another thing that happened to me, I was campused right away.

We stayed in Cavanagh Hall; that's where the athletic offices are and it was a pretty tough, regimented dorm. As freshmen we were supposed to be in every night at ten o'clock in our rooms for bed check. One night in the week we could stay out to eleven. When you became a sophomore you got two midnights a week and you had to be in at ten the rest of the week. In your junior and senior years you had no bed checks. But that freshman year was very restrictive.

So the first weekend I got to go home, I came back to Notre Dame with some Louisville boys who were juniors and seniors. And it was eleven o'clock when I got to the dorm. The priest on my floor—they have a priest on every floor—asked, "What gives?" And I told him I was with these other fellows.

"I don't care who you were with," he said. "You were an hour late." So I was campused. I couldn't leave campus for a month.

That was the time I was dating a little girl from Louisville, then a sophomore in high school; a very pretty little girl named Janie Beackler. I dated her all that year and I was very, very close to her family and I thought that eventually Janie and I might get married. And I missed her.

I'm sure the Notre Dame authorities knew what the freshmen went through because they did try to help us. In addition to tutors where needed, the football players each had a varsity man assigned to him. He was supposed to be like a big brother, one guy on the team who's supposed to look after problems that arise. And Johnny Lattner was assigned to me. Johnny was a halfback and made All-America that year and he won the Heisman Trophy. Since then, he and I have become good friends. He has a restaurant in Chicago now and I try to drop in and see him when I'm there. That fall, Johnny always told me, "If there's anything I can do, if you need something or want to ask me about something, be sure that you do." But I never felt it was right to bother him, to go to him with my troubles.

So that was the state we were in. We had passed up a lot to come here and we naturally hadn't come to maybe sit on the bench and we didn't know whether we were going to get to play here or what. I think every freshman worries about that, but maybe we were worrying a little more than normal.

Naturally, in freshman football you're not seeing any action. You're just out there every day. It seems kind of useless, and I thought that maybe I had made a mistake because I could have gone to Kentucky and played my first year. I felt like I was wasting a year, really wasting a year.

And I had hurt my elbow and Sipes had hurt his knee and we were really down. I don't think it was being homesick so much as it was trying to accustom yourself to a new life.

And we were having trouble accustoming ourselves and that's when we got the idea—the thing that always goes through a freshman's head—well, let's write a letter. So we actually composed a letter to the University of Miami about the possibility of transferring. But we never mailed it, thank heavens.

Then one thing happened to help make me feel better about Notre Dame.

I think anybody who goes to a movie, or watches television, or sees something that is very moving, something that moves you greatly, gets an intense personal reaction. There are spine-tingling effects and you feel like your blood is getting warm. Well, that happened to me at my first pep rally at Notre Dame. I don't think I'll ever forget that.

It was before the opening game against Oklahoma, and there were six thousand students cheering for maybe twelve straight minutes for the team. Then each of the players would be introduced and before the place quieted down it maybe took the speaker five minutes to get to speak. It was really something to see. I was never sure about the spirit on campus until then. At Notre Dame on campus the fellows are a very close-knit group, I found out, even though it didn't seem they were.

The most emotional pep rally I can ever remember came later that year after we had tied Iowa, 14–14. That was the game where they said we had faked injuries to stop the clock in the last moments of both halves. And in that game, Dom Penza, the captain, had dropped two touchdown passes.

Naturally, the captain always gives a speech at every pep rally. Well, Dom Penza got up and his first words were, "I just want to say personally that I'm sorry." And that's all he got to say. And they cheered for thirty-eight minutes—thirty-eight solid minutes. They wouldn't let him say anything. And he was crying, and everybody in the whole joint was crying.

After that we worked harder at trying to adjust to college life, and there were two men who helped me particularly. One was Ralph Guglielmi. Ralph was the junior quarterback when I entered Notre Dame and he went on to become All-America the next year. So naturally we were kind of thrown together, especially in the spring practice of 1954, when I began to work out with the varsity. And he kind of took care of me and we became good friends, and we are good friends today. He got married a couple of years ago and I was an usher at his wedding.

I know the next year we set a record—Sipes and Ralph and Joe Heap, the Heaper, who played halfback. We went to thirty straight movies together. Every night we went into town to the movies.

And through Ralph I got to know Julius Tucker. He's a businessman in South Bend and a rabid Notre Dame football fan and he's always been very good to the players. He's handled over a hundred kids' contracts with the pros coming out of Notre Dame and he helped negotiate mine with Green Bay. He's not a lawyer or anything; actually, all he had was a sixth-grade education. But he's just a wonderful Jewish man who loves Notre Dame. He and Coach Leahy were close friends and he'd always take care of you when you were at Notre Dame. He'd lend you a car or take you to dinner and you'd always go over to the house for Thanksgiving dinner. He'd try to make sure the kids were happy.

So Ralph took me over to Julius's house and Julius and I became friends. I think Ralph and I were two of the closest kids he ever had; at least he always said we were. He was just a beautiful man.

That spring of my freshman year, working out with the varsity, I began to recover my old bounce, my old confidence. I was getting accustomed to the school and now it looked like I would get to play for Notre Dame. I might have even gotten a little cocky. I remember one afternoon I came up to Blackie Johnson, one of our coaches. "Coach," I said, looking real grim, "it looks like tough sledding."

"What do you mean?" All sorts of things probably went through his mind. Was I worried about the team? Did I have a hidden injury?

"Yeah, tough sledding," I grinned. "No snow." That was the kind of wit I had, the knock-'em-over-the-head kind.

The biggest boost to my confidence, one of my biggest thrills ever, actually, came on May 15 that spring when we played the Old-Timers' Game.

That one is usually a war. The old-timers from Notre Dame are like no old-timers from any other school. They are, most of them, ex-All-Americas or guys playing professional football and they come to play. We always have a big crowd for the game, and this one was no exception. My mother had come in for it. (She told someone before the game, "I'm afraid I'll drop dead when he runs out on that field. Maybe I belong home saying the rosary.") My uncle was there and lots of other friends.

I was very jumpy. Coach didn't start me and waiting to get in seemed like forever. In fact the first quarter seemed so long that when it was over I thought the half had ended and I got up and almost started for the dressing room.

I finally got in in the third period; I think we were leading by a point at the time. I was pretty nervous before we ran the first play. But not afterwards.

I played about fifteen minutes all told, about ten on offense. I got to run the ball three times, once on the keep play and twice when I was trapped trying to pass, and I picked up thirty-two yards rushing. I completed five of six passes for 111 yards. Three were for touchdowns, passes of thirty-one, ten, and forty-one yards. One pass gave us a 22–13 lead. Then they caught us and went ahead 26–22 and I passed to Bob Scannell for a touchdown. I kicked two out of three extra points. We beat the old-timers 49–26 and I had had a hand in twenty of our points.

The next day in the Louisville *Courier-Journal,* sportswriter Tommy Fitzgerald started out his story this way: "The famed golden dome of Notre Dame's campus had a young

rival today—a golden-haired football player named Paul
Hornung, who had everybody taking notice of his shining
play."

I think that was the birth of the "Golden Boy," and
Tommy Fitzgerald gets the credit. I felt like Golden Boy all
right, walking off the field after that game. I remember
Guglielmi was the first one to come over and shake my hand.
He was going to be first-string quarterback the next fall and
he might have been nervous about my showing, but he was
all smiles, and with a quip to match.

"Paul," he grinned, "you sure did good, but you didn't
have to do that good."

6. ADVENTURES OF THE "BERSERK ELEPHANT"

Starting the fall semester at Notre Dame as a sophomore in 1954, I felt better about a lot of things. I had made the varsity for one. I didn't expect to play much because there were two first-class senior quarterbacks ahead of me, Ralph Guglielmi and Tom Carey. But I knew I would play some.

Also, my grades had begun to straighten out. I went to summer school for extra courses and did well enough and I knew then that I wouldn't have to worry about flunking.

And now there was no more uncertainty on my part about Notre Dame, no thought about transferring somewhere else.

But some uncertainties did remain.

For one thing, Frank Leahy had quit because of ill health and now Terry Brennan was the new coach. I missed Leahy. He had always been real great to me and, naturally, he was a terrific salesman. But I liked Terry Brennan, too. He had been my freshman coach and we got along real fine. I would say that with what I know now, that Terry Brennan was an excellent coach. He prepared for games carefully, he coached carefully, he handled the players carefully. Terry was fired in 1958 and it was the old story. He was a loser. They don't care who you are, if you don't have the horses, it's awful tough to win. And surely a great coach can make a great team out of a good team. But no coach can make a good team out of a bad team.

Another thing I had to learn that fall was how to play defense. According to the college rules then in force, you had to play both ways. I hadn't played defense in high school but I just went out and played it in college. I *had* to play it. It was a big change but I wasn't the smallest guy in the world and I still wasn't the slowest guy in the world.

By then I was full-grown, six feet two, and maybe 195 pounds, or fifteen pounds less than what I weight today, but with the same essential physical elements. The reason I've been called "Goat" ever since college is because I have no shoulders. Lots of people think it's a gesture of ego when they see me pushing up my shoulder straps on the field, but I have to do it or the damn things will slip down. I'm built like a triangle, as a guy once said. Most of my strength is in my thighs and legs, and neck, too. But not that much from the shoulders to my waist.

My speed then surprised a lot of people because I never looked like I was going fast. I liked to pick my spots. I once beat my teammate Aubrey Lewis in a forty-yard sprint. For a while he held the record for the 400-meter hurdles and he almost made the 1956 Olympic team. I could stay with him for forty yards but he beat me by five yards at 100. He could run the 100 in about 9.8. He'd just glide out.

I was big enough and fast enough, anyway, so that Coach Brennan could work me out at fullback.

Don Schaefer was the starting fullback and a good one, but Terry didn't have too much depth behind him so he came up to me one afternoon and asked if I would switch positions for the team's sake. Naturally, I was glad to. So Terry sent me to the far end of the practice field to report to line coach Bill Walsh for some work on pass blocking.

I'll never forget that afternoon. I kept picking myself up

1. Hornung in Indian suit bought by his Uncle Henry in Green Bay, Wisconsin, about twenty years before Hornung became the leading citizen of Green Bay.

2. Paul Hornung, age seven and a half, third-grader at St. Patrick's School.

3. A senior at Flaget High in Louisville, Hornung had just been named No. 1 high school football player in the state of Kentucky.

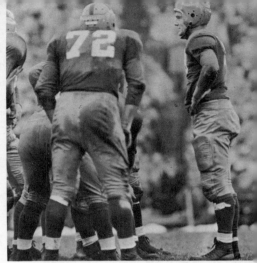

The only two seniors returning to the Notre Dame varsity in the fall of 1956 — football captain Jim Morse and All-America quarterback Hornung. As juniors, Morse and Hornung played on a team that compiled an 8–2 record. Later, Hornung and Morse had dinner together and Hornung said, "Wouldn't it be funny if we were 2–8 next year?" That's what happened. *Courtesy of* Sport *Magazine.*

Hornung won the Heisman Trophy in 1956 as the season's outstanding college football player, the fifth Notre Dame man so honored up to then and only the second to be chosen from a losing team. *Wide World Photo.*

5. Hornung was a one-man team for Notre Dame in 1956. He finished second in the country among college players in total yardage, led Notre Dame in eight different categories. But he was proudest of one category he finished second in—most tackles. *Courtesy of* Sport *Magazine.*

7. "Paul was recruited for Notre Dame by his mother without the strenuous objection of President Theodore Hesburgh and Coach Terry Brennan."

8. On December 4, 1960, against the Chicago Bears, Hornung broke Don Hutson's season scoring record of 138 points. Golden Boy went on to score 176 points for the season. *Wide World Photo.*

9. Hornung scoring against San Francisco, 1960. "I think," Hornung says, "...I would rather score a touchdown on a particular day than make love to the prettiest girl in the United States." *Vernon J. Biever Photo.*

10. No. 5 with Packer head coach Vince Lombardi. "Coach Lombardi's system was fabulous. There was a reason for everything he did." *Vernon J. Biever Photo.*

11. Hornung's closest friend and roommate on the Packers, fellow bachelor Max McGee. "We've always liked the same things. He likes girls, and nice clothes, and nice times and entertainment. He's free with a dollar, I mean he'll go for anything. He's a real swinging guy." *Wide World Photo.*

12. Hornung's big play with Green Bay—the option. It starts as an end sweep and Hornung has the option to pass or run. *Vernon J. Biever Photo.*

off the ground time after time. I got belted around pretty good. My face was a mess. Terry came over, looked at me, and grinned.

"Learn anything?" he asked.

"Sure," I said. "You hit them before they hit you."

We had to go some in 1954 to live up to the record of the 1953 team, which didn't lose a game, and had only that 14–14 tie with Iowa. Most of the experts were predicting before the season that Notre Dame would be one of the top three teams in the country, and we did have a strong squad.

Our first game was with Texas and Coach told me that if we kicked off, I would do the kicking. Naturally, I got a bad case of butterflies, since it was my first varsity ball game. Just before kickoff, Guglielmi, that seasoned veteran, came up to me, to "cheer me up."

"Wouldn't it be funny," he said, "if we lost the toss and you had to kick off and went up there before fifty-nine thousand people, all the publicity and everything, and you missed the ball."

I said, "Well, you're a fine guy. Now you want me to start thinking about that."

And we did lose the toss and I did have to kick off. But I didn't miss the ball, thank God.

I played only about three minutes of that game. I got in one offensive play at quarterback. I handed off to Dick Fitzgerald and he went for nine yards. And we beat Texas, 21–0.

The next week against Purdue, our non-losing streak was busted at thirteen games. We lost, 27–14. Len Dawson made his debut against us and threw four touchdown passes. My biggest piece of action came when I took a kickoff and ran it back sixty yards.

About this time another assistant coach, Bill Early, gave me the nickname, "Dancing Bear." Sherrill was called "Ridge Runner" and Early found out I liked to dance and everything. And in practice one day at quarterback, I hopped over to hand off instead of sliding smoothly, and from then on I was the "Dancing Bear." Until my junior year, that is, when I broke my nose in a game and was given a new nickname—"the Honker."

We beat Pittsburgh in the third game, 33–0, and Brennan gave the sophomores a chance to play. Sherrill had his best game. He caught a touchdown pass from Tom Carey. I scored the fourth touchdown faking a pass and bootlegging eleven yards. I also intercepted a pass on our goal line.

After the Michigan State game, which we won 20–19, I began to play fullback. We were ahead 6–0 against Navy and they were moving late in the game but I intercepted a pass on our seventeen. I gained twenty-nine yards in six carries and got off one forty-one yard punt.

We won our next two games big, 42–7 over Penn and 42–13 over North Carolina, and that was my biggest game as a sophomore. It was actually the first game I played quite a bit. I played the whole second half at quarterback. I completed five passes and carried seven times for seventy-two yards, including a thirty-eight-yard bootleg play. I ran seventy yards with an intercepted pass, but they caught me from behind on the one-yard line and did I catch hell for that!

Early the next week in practice, George Dixon, the quarterback coach, ranted and raved at me. "Never again will that ever happen, Hornung." George is a real character, a real great guy. But he took me out on the field after practice and I had to get down into the three-point stance on the goal line and he'd blow the whistle and I'd sprint, and he'd blow the whistle and I'd stop and get down right away. Sprint and stop, sprint and stop. And I went up and down the field five or six, maybe eight times. About the eighth time I couldn't go down any more and I fell down. And George got

me on my feet and made me go again. I think I crawled off
the practice field that day. The only thought I had then was,
"Are you kidding me?" And the dream I had that night was
Dixon saying, "It'll never happen again." So ever since then,
they've always had that whistle drill at Notre Dame.

We went on to beat Iowa, Southern California, and Southern Methodist and ended with a 9–1 season. Altogether I
played 113 minutes, scored eighteen points, punted six times
for an average of thirty-nine yards a kick, ran twenty-three
times for an average of 6.9 a carry, and intercepted three
passes.

Then I rushed out for basketball.

I didn't think I would make the squad since the season
was already under way, but I did squeeze in as sixth or
seventh man. As a sophomore I started a few games and
you could always know one thing, I wasn't bashful about
shooting. I was a gunner, you know. I got sixty-one points
in ten games and that ended my basketball career. There
was just too much pressure on me scholastically and they
wanted me to quit basketball, anyway, so I did.

When you're playing sports at Notre Dame, it's about 50
per cent practice and 50 per cent study and that makes 100
per cent and leaves no time for anything else. And I liked to
do other things, too, like date girls. But I just didn't have too
much time those first two years at Notre Dame. After practice was over you were too tired and beat and you had your
studies to get with. So there were only Saturday nights,
really, and once in a while a weekend at home. But I didn't
care much. I was really gung-ho those days about making
good in football.

The summer between my sophomore and junior years,
Sherrill and I worked for a brewing company in Louisville
loading and unloading beer kegs. Which was good conditioning. And when I had time, I'd go out to the Flaget High

practice field and punt. I'd punt the ball from one end of
the field to the other. Kick, trot down the field, get the ball,
kick it back. I'd do that hours at a time and it helped my
kicking and it helped my leg muscles.

When I reported for practice in late August of 1955 I
would have to say that I was in the best condition of my life.
I was ready. The team was ready, too.

We had been hit hard by graduation. Goog and Carey
were gone, which left the quarterback job open to me; and
we had lost a lot of other good boys. We also lost a lot of
men to injuries. When I was a freshman we had a freshman
squad of sixty-five. When I was a sophomore we had about
fifteen knee injuries. Another ten or eleven flunked out. By
the time I was a senior, there were only two of those sixty-
five left—Jim Morse and myself.

That fall most of the experts picked us to have a 6–4 record, at best. Coach Brennan wasn't very optimistic. The only
optimist was Frank Leahy and he could afford to be, he
wasn't coaching any more. "That Hornung," Leahy told a
writer in that spectacular prose of his, "runs like a mower
going through grass. Tacklers just fall off him. His passing is
tops and his kicking is, too. Why, when he reported to me as
a freshman, he could punt eighty yards and place-kick over
the crossbar from seventy yards."

That description was almost as wild as the writer who
said, "Hornung runs like a berserk elephant trampling
through a banana patch."

Wouldn't it be nice if it were that easy. But it was a re-
warding season in every respect.

We played the whole season actually with about sixteen
ballplayers and that was the real test of the thing. If we
could have won our last ball game against Southern Cal, our
record would have been the best of any Notre Dame team
ever, considering the ballplayers we had that year. Ray Le-

mek, our captain, played on one leg, but he just played his heart out all year. Our other guard, Pat Bisceglia, had a bad leg all year. We had one center and one center alone, Jim Mense. Gene Kapish, our end, had a bad knee and played the whole year. And we didn't have too many substitutes. We just played the same group game in and game out, and if they got hurt they played the next week, anyway.

Our opening game in 1955 was against Southern Methodist and there was quite a bit of publicity in Louisville because two Louisville boys were going to start for Notre Dame— Sipes and Hornung. Sipes took the opening kickoff and ran it back to the twenty and got hit in the mouth and blood was coming out and when he came back to the huddle I looked at him and said, "Doggone it, you got hit already?"

But we went on from there, driving right down and scoring. I went the last eleven yards on the option. I also kicked my first college field goal, thirty-five yards, with Sipes holding. We beat S.M.U., 17–0.

We beat Indiana in the next game 19–0 and I scored one touchdown on a thirty-three-yard end run, and passed to Dick Prendergast for the other. I got to intercept a pass, too.

We beat Miami, 14–0. I passed for both the touchdowns and got off one fifty-one yard punt.

So going to the Michigan State game we were unbeaten, untied and unscored upon and, naturally, they had us as the No. 1 team in the country.

But Michigan State beat us 21–7, and that was a tough one to take.

We scored first when I hit Jim Morse on a forty-yard pass. Then Clarence Peaks took my punt and raced it back seventy yards and I just managed to bring him down, but it set up their touchdown, anyway. In the third quarter with their fullback, Gerry Planutis, doing the heavy-duty work, they went eighty yards for the touchdown. They scored the clincher in the fourth period after they recovered a fumble.

Terry got us back up for Purdue, though. We wanted that one badly, anyway, because of what they had done to us the year before. And we won, 22–7. I didn't do much on offense in that game, though I did recover a Purdue fumble and intercepted a pass. That's the game they broke my nose. I was running back a kickoff. There was a pileup. I got up groggy. On the sidelines they jerked the nose back straight, stuffed cotton up it to stop the bleeding, and when I went back in the huddle one of the boys looked at me and said, "Oh, hell, there goes Hornung's Hollywood contract."

The next game we played Navy and actually that was the day I made All-America.

I was having a great year up to that game and so was the Navy quarterback, George Welsh, and so the sportswriters billed it as Welsh against Hornung. Everybody knows in football, if the Eastern sportswriters are behind you, you're going to make All-America. It's as simple as that. They carry more power than anybody.

And Welsh didn't have one of his greatest days. He had a good day, but I had a very good day—passing, running, and playing defense.

There was the usual crowd at South Bend for the game, fifty-nine thousand-plus, and they enjoyed themselves. They watched Welsh complete thirteen of twenty-five passes, while we were keeping the ball mainly on the ground. I ran twenty-four yards to the Navy one, then scored on a sneak. Aubrey Lewis scored our second touchdown. Then I intercepted a Navy pass and threw to Gene Kapish for thirty-six yards. We beat Navy 21–7 and the Eastern writers gave me a lot of good publicity after that.

We won our next two games, beating Penn 46–14 and North Carolina, 27–7. Then we played Iowa and I would have to call that one the most satisfying game of my college career.

We were losing 14–7 with about seven minutes to go, and we started moving the football. I took the kickoff up the middle for twenty-three yards to our thirty-seven. I hit on a seventeen-yard pass to Kapish, then a fifteen-yarder to Prendergast, to the Iowa thirty-one. Then Dick Fitzgerald went up the middle for fifteen more. I tried a short pass, which was incomplete. The next play was supposed to be a screen pass to the right. But the Iowa linemen poured in. I dodged one tackler, sidestepped another, and started retreating to the left. Finally from about my forty, I spotted Jim Morse in the end zone. He was supposed to be our faking receiver on the play, but he was all alone. I hit him deep in the end zone and it was a tie game.

The next time we got the ball there was a little over four minutes left, on the Iowa forty-three. First play I missed a pass. The next one Dean Studer went into the line for four yards. Then I carried down to their thirty but the play was called back because of a penalty. That made it third and eleven and, baby, everything was on the line. I went back, spotted Morse, and Jim made a great catch, taking it away from two defenders on the nine-yard line, a thirty-five-yard gain. Fitzgerald tried the line for no gain. Studer went around end for five yards. On third down, I was dropped on the line of scrimmage. So it was fourth and goal, and one of the coaches threw in the kicking tee and we were penalized fifteen yards for "coaching from the sidelines."

I was very excited when we lined up for the field goal try. I had never been so tense and nervous before. I remember exactly what was on my mind just before I tried the kick. I was thinking of that game my senior year in high school when we played Chattanooga Central, when I had tried a field goal with the score 7–7, and missed. Just before the kick against Iowa, standing back there alone, I kept repeating to myself, "Let's not have another Chattanooga game. . . . Let's not have another Chattanooga game."

Jim Morse held on the Iowa eighteen, which made it a twenty-eight-yarder. He placed the ball perfectly, the line held, and I kicked and it went through.

And after the game my teammates and some of the fans carried me off the field. It was a wonderful feeling, I'll tell you that.

The next week on the Coast against Southern Cal, I had another big game, but it wasn't nearly as satisfying. We lost. And when you lose, I don't care how big a game you have personally, you don't feel elated over it.

Walking off the field at halftime in that game, I was dead. After the game I don't think I ever felt as tired about a college game. I played fifty-nine minutes, offense and defense, and they were scoring as fast as we were scoring, and I was running after everybody.

They opened up with a touchdown, then I ran eight yards for a touchdown to even it. Then they picked up two more touchdowns. Then I hit Jim on a seventy-eight-yard pass play and at halftime they had us 21–13.

The third quarter was scoreless, though I got off a fifty-nine-yard run on the keeper. In the fourth quarter I hit Morse again on a sixty-yarder and that set up the touchdown and put us just one point behind, 21–20. But U.S.C. exploded for three closing touchdowns. Jon Arnett went sixty-four yards for one, and ninety-five thousand fans went home satisfied, at least the U.S.C. fans did.

I had had quite a game statistically. I gained 259 yards passing and ninety-five running and that total of 354 was the most accumulated in a single game in 1955 by any college player.

So we ended with an 8–2 record, which was still a lot

better than had been predicted. Considering the circumstances, it was one of the best seasons in Notre Dame's history. It was a good season personally, too. My total yardage—1215—was fourth highest in the country. I led the club in passing, with forty-six completions in 103 tries for 743 yards; I led in punting, thirty punts for an average of thirty-four yards each; I led in scoring, forty-six points; and finished second in rushing (ninety-two carries for 472 yards) and second in kickoff returns. And I made a lot of the big All-America teams.

Shortly after the season, Jim Morse and I were having dinner together and we talked about how nice it was to win eight games out of ten. And, jokingly, I said to him, "Wouldn't it be funny if we were 2–8 next year?"

Some joke.

7. A LUAU FOR THE HEISMAN WINNER

My senior year at Notre Dame was a crazy-quilt mixture of the good and the bad. On the bad side was the fact that we had a losing season. I was very, very surprised after the season was over that I had won as many honors as I did. There was great personal satisfaction in that, but as I have said, I'd much rather do well personally for a winning team.

On the good side was the fact that I had a lot more freedom than I ever had. As a freshman and sophomore I hardly ever got out. My schedule improved as a junior and by the time I was a senior it worked out very well. You're allowed three cuts in each course, so after you find your way around you start to know—to save your cuts for a particular weekend and maybe miss Monday and Tuesday classes and you make a long weekend out of it.

I never had any weekend classes my senior year. Because I had gone to summer school that one time, I was five or six credits ahead. It was a school rule that you had to have a minimum of twelve to fifteen hours a semester, no matter how many credits you were ahead. So I had the minimum amount of hours my senior year and that gave me plenty of free weekends. And my school work never suffered. I was averaging 82 at the School of Commerce.

That's why all those stories that came out about my so-called off-campus activities were so exaggerated. I never snuck off campus as much as people said I did, because I didn't have to; I had all the free time, anyway. Actually, when you become a senior you know the ropes pretty well. I don't think there's ever been a kid who's gone all the way through Notre Dame who didn't sneak out once in a while; just for the mere fact that they have a rule against it, naturally, you're gonna have to try and break it.

But I never snuck out when I was a junior and only a few times as a senior. I had a car a lot, you know. Julius Tucker let me borrow his car, and that was definitely against the rules—to drive a car while on campus. And one night I almost got caught.

I was parked way down by the stadium just before curfew when the father who was the prefect of discipline saw those headlights go on and got in his car and started to drive down to investigate. I took off in my car—I only had fifteen minutes to make it back to the dorm—and he took off after me. It was a good thing my car was a little faster than his. I doubled back fast and parked the car, and had to run a mile and just barely made it by twelve o'clock curfew.

And, naturally, being from Notre Dame, I began to get a lot of fan mail, especially a lot of mail from girls. They'd send me their pictures, for me to call them I supposed. By the time I was a senior I was getting so much mail that I turned the answering job over to this little friend of mine. His name was Eddie and I won't embarrass him now to give his last name. He was in pre-law at the time and he was a real sharp guy and he liked football.

Eddie was quite a letter-writer. These girls would write me and he would write maybe a two-page answer. He was so intense in doing this that he sometimes got me into trouble and once, answering a girl's letter, he got me into deep trouble. I'll go into that later.

So I began to get in the columns when I was a senior. After the season I attended a few winter carnivals and things. I figured I could go up to those winter resorts and have a nice time. I'd never been skiing in my life and I thought I might enjoy it. The one time I agreed to go up to a New York resort, this movie starlet was queen of the carnival, and I was hoping we'd have a helluva time. We got up there and it rained and they had to import the snow and it was just a terrible weekend. I was glad to get out of there.

Most of my weekends, though, I spent in Chicago. I got to love that town. I had this pretty girl there, and I'd go out and have dinner with somebody and we'd be in the London House with this one and that, and I began to get my name in the gossip columns. I began to get a lot of publicity.

And of course it was being a Notre Dame quarterback that was responsible, and winning the Heisman Trophy that senior year with a team that lost eight ball games.

After I made all those All-America teams in my junior year, I thought some about the Heisman Trophy, which is voted on by the nation's sportswriters and sportscasters, voted annually to the best college football player in the country. I felt that if I had a good year, I would win it. It was just a dream, naturally. I realized that there's one magic thing about Notre Dame—it's the magic thing about the quarterbacks of Notre Dame. If you're winning and you're a good one, you get more publicity than maybe a great one at another school.

But I never thought I could win the thing with a losing team.

It was just a combination of things. We had so many sophomores in '56 and you just can't play the type of schedule we played with inexperienced ballplayers. Naturally, a sophomore is going to make a lot of mistakes. Also, a lot of the older kids didn't come through as well as expected.

We opened against Southern Methodist and were fourteen-point favorites, but we got beat, 19–13. It was the first opening-day loss for Notre Dame since 1934. We almost caught them, though. We were losing 13–0 when I passed to Jim Morse for fifty-five yards and then kicked the extra point. Then with ten minutes left we had a fourth and three situation on our own forty-three. I ran fifty-seven yards for a touchdown, but the extra point was blocked. Two minutes later they scored again. I ended up with 101 yards rushing and 136 yards passing, but it wasn't enough. And that started it all out.

The next week we beat Indiana, 20–6. I completed nine of fifteen passes for 121 yards and rushed for eighty-one yards. Aubrey Lewis ran for our third touchdown.

And that was our last victory until my last home game at South Bend.

Purdue beat us 28–14. I threw two touchdown passes, ran a kickoff back fifty-nine yards, but Purdue intercepted one of my passes that set up their winning touchdown.

Against Michigan State, the next week, I got my first serious injury as a college player.

It was a tough 7–7 game at halftime, and I had passed for our only touchdown. Starting the second half I kicked off to Michigan State and a fast kid by the name of Dennis Mendyk got loose and I was the only one between him and the goal line and got him on a shoestring tackle; but I dislocated my left thumb diving for him. I stayed in and ended up with a total yardage of 209 yards, but they walloped us 47–14. Sherrill Sipes, who had a bad knee all year long, scored our other touchdown.

The next week we played Oklahoma and that was awful. They were rated No. 1 in the country and when I went out

there for our first scrimmage play I knew we were in trouble.
I looked up and down the line and our young kids were
shaking. They were just very nervous. I carried on the first
play for five yards, then carried again for the first down.
And after that we didn't get anywhere and they beat us
40-0, and intercepted four of my passes.

Navy beat us 33-7 and I dislocated my right thumb and
it was very difficult to pass. Against Pittsburgh I started at
fullback. I ran for a fifty-yard touchdown, then took an interception back fifty-six yards, but Pitt beat us, 26-13.

About this time there was some criticism of me for calling
my own plays so often. Well, I don't know what else I could
have done. Naturally, we ran the option play a lot and if
the end didn't tackle me, I'd run the ball. And we'd get
behind and I'd have to pass. Naturally, if you're back to pass
on a third and long situation, if you can complete the pass
you're a hero and the guy that catches it is a hero. But there
weren't many Notre Dame heroes those afternoons.

My last home game for Notre Dame was to be against
North Carolina and naturally I wanted it to be an extra-
special one. The sportswriters billed it as a duel between
Eddie Sutton and myself. Eddie was a fast, shifty halfback
who was having a great season. And he did have a good day
against us, running for 136 yards on twenty-one carries and
completing three of five passes for 140 yards. But I had a
good day, too.

Because of my sore thumbs, Terry Brennan devised some
special formations. At times I operated out of the halfback
slot, other times out of the fullback slot. We took a quick
14-0 lead and I scored both touchdowns on short-yardage
situations. Then they came back to tie the score. With
seventy-six seconds left, I scored the third touchdown and
we beat them, 21-14. I had carried eighteen times for
ninety-one yards, completed four of eleven passes for 103

yards, kicked three times for a thirty-nine-yard average. And for the second time in my college career, I was carried off the field. I still have in my scrapbook back home a piece of the goal post from that game that someone sent me.

But my thumb was still pretty bad and I didn't play much against Iowa. They beat us 48–8. My final college game was to be on the Coast against Southern California and naturally it had to be enveloped in a hassle.

I had come back to the dorm one night and Julius Tucker was there, waiting for me. "Paul," he said, "Coach Leahy wants you to be on his television show."

Leahy was going to present the All-America team and it was to be a nationwide television show. Tucker said, "He's willing to pay your mother's way to California if you'll be on the show."

It was an eight o'clock show and it would take about fifteen minutes and I told Julius it sounded good to me.

He said, "Well, you have to get Coach Brennan's permission."

So I went to talk to Terry. He said, "First of all, Paul, you know the rules—nobody goes on any television right before a game while we're on a trip."

I said, "I understand, but . . ."

He interrupted. "It was a rule that Leahy put in himself when he was here. He told me that if he was the coach, he'd jump out of his skin if his players went on television before a game."

"I understand, coach, but . . ."

"Secondly," Terry continued, "this television show goes on all over the country, and it goes on at eleven o'clock in the East and Midwest. We're not having too good a year and I think we'd get a lot of criticism having one of our players *seem* to be out late the night before a game."

Terry was apologetic but firm. "Sure, I'd like for you to go on. I want to see you do it, but I can't."

So I told him I understood and I sent Coach Leahy a telegram that I couldn't make it due to the rules and regulations. And he got kind of peeved and sounded off about Notre Dame's team "lacking the spirit of former Notre Dame teams."

Well, I felt that was a bad rap. At no time during the season did we feel we were laying down. Nobody likes to have anybody think he's laying down. We were trying in every game. And I felt that Brennan was doing the best he could considering the circumstances. I think actually that he did as good or better a job in 1956 as he did with our winning team in 1955. We had all those sophomores, and injuries killed us, too, for heaven's sake. And we just couldn't function well.

That blast really got us up against Southern California. They were heavily favored and we almost beat them. Bob Williams played quarterback and did a helluva job. I played halfback and ran back a kickoff ninety-five yards for one touchdown. But Williams passed brilliantly and they just did beat us, 28–20. And after the game Frank Leahy told the press, "It was Notre Dame's best game of the year."

Unfortunately, it was still the worst season in Notre Dame history and by this time I had forgotten all about my Heisman Trophy chances even though I had had a good season personally. I finished second in the country in total yardage to John Brodie, with 1337 yards. I had 420 yards rushing in ninety-four carries, completed fifty-nine of 111 passes for 917 yards (but I also had thirteen interceptions). All told I led Notre Dame in eight different categories. I was especially proud of one category that I finished second in—the most tackles. I made fifty-five tackles that year.

On the morning of December 6 I was still in my dorm when I got a call from Tom Harmon, the ex-Michigan All-America and now a network television announcer.

"Congratulations, Paul," he said.

"For what?" I was curious.

"For winning the Heisman Trophy."

I nearly fell off my chair. I really couldn't believe it. That was the greatest thrill of my life, being named the outstanding college football player of the country, and the first thing I did when I recovered was call Mom and tell her.

Then I did a round of celebrating, which was interrupted a little bit by two postseason bowl games. I played in the East-West game in San Francisco and had a pretty good day though we lost, 7–6. Then I went out to Honolulu for the Hula Bowl game and that was the most swinging time of my life up to then.

I got blamed for a few things that happened there, but nothing was my fault . . . though I did kind of instigate things.

Jim Morse, Jon Arnett and myself all took the penthouse on top of the Reef Hotel in Honolulu. The Hula Bowl officials had told us, "We don't mind how much you spend for food and a few drinks. Only thing you can't buy is clothes."

And I said, "Well, that's all right." And we figured the only way to do things right in Hawaii was to throw our own luau and invite everybody in town. So we rented the whole side of the hotel downstairs and we had our own little luau. And that was the night before the game.

It was a great week. It was probably the only time, I would imagine, that college football players ever relaxed during a week of practice for a game. We would go over to practice from the beach in bathing trunks. We'd just put on tennis shoes and run around in our trunks. Then we would go right back to the beach. We had long thirty-five-minute practices each day.

And we invited all the girls we knew to our luau. I knew an airline stewardess from Minnesota who was working in Honolulu. And I met another girl through Frank Sennes, who was the owner of the Moulin Rouge in L.A. And we had about fifteen or twenty girls there and we had everything —Hawaiian punch, Polynesian food, bands and music and dancing, the whole thing. Everybody wandered out during the evening. Honolulu never closes, you know, and it was the first time in my life that I had ever gone out the night before a game.

I don't know what happened but I got to sleep about two hours on the beach and I woke up about eight-thirty or nine when the sun hit me in the face.

Naturally, I had to rush like hell to make the game. The starting backfield was Tommy McDonald at right halfback, Jim Swink at fullback, John Brodie at quarterback, me at left half. Brodie and I were going to switch off and I figured I could take it easy awhile, and I needed to because I was beat. But Brodie got hurt on one of the first plays, on a dive play. I always kidded him that he really did take a dive because it was too hot and he didn't want to play. But he got racked pretty good. So I had to play quarterback the whole way and it was hot, oh it was hot. It was ninety and I about died.

There I was, not knowing what the hell was going on. I remember in the huddle I drew a play on the ground, like they do in sandlot. "Here's what we're gonna do!" I said. "We're gonna run a bootleg. Everyone run one way, I'm gonna run the other."

I was supposed to pass but no one was on my side and I ran the ball and I broke loose and went about sixty-five yards and couldn't go any farther and the best thing that ever happened to me was that somebody tackled me from behind. I had to lay there for about six minutes to get my breath to get up. Nobody else could play quarterback, so they had to call two time outs in a row.

But I had a pretty good day. I threw once to Joe Walton for a thirty-four-yard touchdown. I threw to Arnett, who lateraled to Tommy McDonald for a touchdown. I threw to Jimmy Morse, who raced fifty-three yards. I hit on ten of twenty-one passes for 168 yards and all three of our touchdowns. I rushed the ball five times for seventy-six yards. The Hawaiian All-Stars—mostly San Francisco 49er and Los Angeles Ram players, and quarterbacked by Norm Van Brocklin—beat us 55–21 but I won a trophy as the game's outstanding back.

The next thing I know I was out at the airport. Jim Morse and I had to get back to school early. I was waiting for the plane at the airport when I heard the loudspeaker: "Paul Hornung, please report to Pan American Airlines."

I was talking to Jimmy and I walked over to the ticket counter. I said, "I'm Paul Hornung. Is there a message for me?"

And there was a sheriff and three policemen standing there and the sheriff said, "We have a bill here from the Reef Hotel for eight hundred dollars for purchase of clothes, and you signed for it."

"I didn't buy any clothes," I protested. And I hadn't.

"Well, here's your signature." It was my name but not my signature. Somebody had gone in and bought some clothes in my name.

I finally talked them into letting me board the plane. I told them when I got back to the States I would send them a check. So they let me leave and eventually I had to pay for the clothes. I kid John Brodie to this day about it. When-

ever I see him I say, "Brodie, you sonofagun, you or Arnett
—one of you two—I know you did it."

But that was quite an outing and every time I look at the
trophy from the Hula Bowl and the certificate they sent me,
I get a chuckle. The certificate reads: "Be it known that Paul
Hornung voluntarily and with cheerful devotion did per-
form meritorious service in the interest of noble humanitar-
ianism for the Hula Bowl Committee."

Of course I had been scouted by the pros while in college
and I knew a lot of the teams were interested in me. Bob
Waterfield scouted me for the Los Angeles Rams and he told
the Rams to try and get me. The New York Giants scouted
me and were interested, and so were a lot of clubs. I also
got an offer from Canada, through Frank Leahy. Vancouver
offered me thirty-five thousand dollars if I signed with them.
But I wanted to play football in the States. As Mom told
one writer, "If I wanted money, I wouldn't have sent my son
to Notre Dame in the first place."

I received one other tempting offer, but not to play football. Twentieth Century-Fox wanted me to sign a contract
with a seven-year option and become a movie actor. I said
no. Then they came up with a set amount; they offered me
twenty-five thousand dollars a year guaranteed. But they
didn't want me to play football. They wanted me to go to
actor's school. I wanted to play football, so that was that.

Actually, if I were going to play in the National Football
League, there was no choice. If I had one I would have
taken the Chicago Bears. Being so close to Chicago and
knowing so many people there and liking the town, anyway.
And the Bears had a helluva football team.

But there were two teams who had a shot at me. The
Chicago Cardinals and Packers had finished in a tie for last
place and had to toss a coin to determine which team would

receive the bonus choice, then in effect in the N.F.L. I knew I was going to one of them. Green Bay won the toss and Lisle Blackbourn, the coach, said, "We take Paul Hornung of Notre Dame." And that was it.

I let Julius Tucker negotiate my contract as he does for a lot of the college seniors, and there wasn't any real problem. Jack Vainisi, the Green Bay business manager and a fine man, flew to Notre Dame in a private plane with six members of the Green Bay Packers' board of directors. And after eight minutes of conversation, I signed the contract.

I got a three-year deal, fifteen thousand dollars a year, plus a three-thousand-dollar bonus. I was no Joe Namath, I got no four hundred thousand dollars. But for those days, it wasn't bad. I was satisfied. And being an optimist and a confident kind of fellow, I felt I wouldn't have any trouble doing the job for the Packers.

But I still had a few things to learn.

Part III

13. Under Lombardi, Hornung, here protecting quarterback Bart Starr, became a proficient blocker. "Coach's philosophy of offense was direct: Try to knock everybody down on every play." *Vernon J. Biever Photo.*

14. In 1961 championship game against the New York Giants, Hornung was named the most valuable player. He credits his guards (No. 63, Fuzzy Thurston here) for much of his success. "If the guards don't block, Hornung doesn't score." *Vernon J. Biever Photo.*

15. With Bart Starr holding, Hornung kicks another field goal. He was unable to explain his 1964 kicking drought except that he likened it to a golfer who was in a temporary slump. *Green Bay Packer Photo by Vernon J. Biever.*

16. Sliding through a hole against the Minnesota Vikings. "I think the thing that always helped my ball-carrying more than anything was intelligence, knowing how to cut and when to cut." *Vernon J. Biever Photo.*

17. Hornung suffered a serious knee injury in a 1962 game against the Minnesota Vikings, played sparingly for the rest of the year. *Wide World Photo.*

18. After missing the 1963 season for betting on football games, Hornung came back in the summer of 1964 determined to be in the best shape of his life. *Vernon J. Biever Photo.*

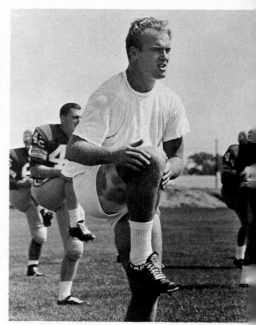

19. An autographed football for two Green Bay citizens. "I'd really love to have kids.... Maybe the perfect thing for me would be not to be married and have kids. That would probably fit the mold better." *Vernon J. Biever Photo.*

20. A fiancée calls. "Of course I want to see you. Whenever you get enough money to come and see me, I want you to come....If I paid your way, I'd feel kind of guilty about it, you know that....Of course I still love you." *Vernon J. Biever Photo.*

1. SOME BONUS PLUM

The way not to start a career in pro football is to have a girl waiting for you on the front steps at your training camp where the coach can see her. That's what happened to me when I reported to Stevens Point, Wisconsin in July of 1957.

Ron Kramer and I drove from Chicago where we had both played (I use the word loosely) in the college All-Star game against the N.F.L. champion New York Giants. We talked about that game and how glad we were it was over with.

It wasn't like the Hula Bowl, I'll tell you that.

First of all, we had an unbelievable squad. You name them, they were there. John Brodie and Len Dawson were the other two quarterbacks. Other 1956 All-Americas were Ron Kramer, Jim Parker, Jerry Tubbs, Bill Glass, Joe Walton, Tommy McDonald, Jim Brown, Paul Wiggin, Alex Karras, Lamar Lundy, Jim Swink, Jon Arnett, Clarence Peaks, Abe Woodson, Jim Podoley, Don Bosseler, Don Shinnick, Del Shofner, Billy Barnes, Alex Sandusky, Henry Jordan. Every last one of them made the pros.

Naturally, you put that kind of a group together for two weeks before the game, you can't just lock everybody up. You had to go down there and have a good time at least a week before the game. I was never the kind of ballplayer to stay in every night. I couldn't play ball that way. I wouldn't be loose. When the weekend came, we wanted to get out. We didn't want to sit around the dormitory week nights, either.

We were camped at Northwestern University in suburban Evanston, Illinois, and a lot of the guys hung around the campus because the girls from Northwestern were such gracious and willing hostesses. Me? I preferred Chicago. I was going with this exotic dancer at the time, and we were making the scene as often as possible. So one night I was out a little late and I fell asleep in this friend's apartment. I woke up and it was like nine-fifteen in the morning and practice was scheduled for nine-thirty and I was thirty miles on the other side of Chicago, and that was quite a long distance to go in fifteen minutes.

I had a little car then, a Ford convertible with an aerial sticking out of the back hose and an engine that burned as much oil as gas. So I didn't make it back to practice in time. I got out on the field and, feeling kind of loose, asked one of the assistant coaches, "What's the latest an All-Star player ever got in after curfew?" He looked at me funny but I couldn't stop. "Whatever it is," I said, "I've broken the record. I just this minute got in."

What was I going to do, lie to him? After that, I was running with the second backfield.

All kinds of ridiculous rumors about me seeped out of Evanston. One was that I was busting out so much that Curly Lambeau, the coach of the All-Stars, had to call Notre Dame to ask for help in keeping me in camp. Well, that was completely fictitious. Curly Lambeau was from Green Bay and I knew he was all for me. I got along real well with him. I maybe didn't get along quite as well those two weeks with the backfield coach, Otto Graham. He made some remarks about me in the paper to the effect that he doubted I could make the pros—period. Actually, he was right if he meant as a quarterback. But he was the backfield coach and I wanted to play in the All-Star game and, reading that, I did have a little bit of mixed emotions about him.

Early in practice I was doing very well. I think we had Jon Arnett, Jim Brown, and myself in the first backfield and we had a pretty good first scrimmage. We moved the ball well. But then I showed up late for that practice and after that I wasn't in the starting backfield anymore. Naturally, I wanted to play and felt bad. But Brodie and Dawson were better passers than me.

The night of the game, which is held at Soldier Field before eighty thousand or so people, twenty-two of our squad ran through the goal posts at game time and were introduced in the floodlights. I wasn't among them. Neither was Jim Brown. We didn't start. I played just a bit the first half and I don't think Jimmy played at all. At halftime Jimmy came over to me.

"Let's get dressed," he said. "You get dressed, I'll get dressed."

"No," I said. "Let's not cause a story. We only got to hang around another thirty minutes."

He was disgusted and I don't blame him. Neither of us played much the second half. The Giants won, 22–12. And that's the reason I was glad to be out of that camp and on the way to join the Packers.

I wouldn't maybe have been quite so happy if I knew what was waiting for me.

Eddie, my letter-writing friend from Notre Dame, had gotten me into hot water.

As I said, a lot of girls were writing me letters my senior year in college, enclosing their picture, too. Eddie was answering them for me and sometimes, if he liked what he saw in one of those photos, he'd get a little too passionate in his replies. Once, one of Eddie's letters was sent back be-

cause it had the wrong address on it. I opened it and read it.
He was really giving her hell—"I love you, darling," and all
that. I was mortified; Eddie put me in a real spot sometimes.

The worst spot was when I got a letter from this girl and
she sent her picture, and it was unbelievable. The girl
looked like Brigitte Bardot. I think Eddie kind of flipped
over her. He sent her a letter, signing my name, telling her
that I would be at Stevens Point, Wisconsin in mid-July and
hoping we could meet there.

Well, she showed up all right, all 198 pounds of her. She
was no Brigitte Bardot, after all. Ron and I drove right out
to practice that first day, suited up, hung around and
watched the regulars, and then got dressed and went to our
dorm. She was waiting outside and Coach Lisle Blackbourn
spotted her.

"What do you want?" he barked.

"I'm waiting for Paul Hornung," she said. "He invited me
here."

Blackbourn blew his top. He ran her off, hollering, "There
won't be any girls in my camp! There won't be any girls in
my camp!" Then he called me in his office.

My first day in camp and I had some explaining to do.

Blackbourn was a big man, a tough-looking fellow who
had a good reputation as a coach. Right away, he gave me
hell.

"Listen," he said, "I know that you've been out and you
know how to handle yourself and you've been around, but
I'm not going to stand for this kind of thing."

I said, "There must be some kind of mistake, Coach. I
don't know the girl. I never talked to her in my life. Heck, I
wouldn't invite a *beautiful* girl here, you know."

"Just watch yourself," he said. "I'm not going to allow any
of this stuff to go on in my camp."

I was dismissed and later Lisle Blackbourn told one of the sportswriters that I was a "smart aleck," and we never did get along 100 per cent after that incident.

But I got along right away with the Packer veterans. They were waiting for me to show up, or maybe *laying* for me is a better way to put it. A few days before I arrived, Bobby Dillon, one of the veteran Packers, got up at dinner in camp and announced: "Only two days to go and big No. 5 will be here."

They were waiting for me all right. Those early scrimmages were beautiful. I got belted around pretty good, but managed to get up with a grin each time. The only thing you can do is come right back to them and laugh with them. And after awhile they accept you. You can always tell the different kinds of kidding. When it's all in fun, it's fun and laughing and everything. But it's a different kind of laughter when they're really digging at you. And there were a lot of rookies who couldn't take it.

At one scrimmage, I was on the wedge team for the kick-off return. They always put the rookies on the wedge team. That's when there are four guys in front of the two back for the kick; they form a wedge and block for whoever takes the ball. So it was myself and Dave Hanner and Jerry Hellunin and Bill Forester. And this hot rookie was coming down fast. Boy, he was wild, and I didn't like the look in his eye.

Lucky for me, he picked out Jerry Hellunin to hit. So I went running by and Jerry went ahead and tried to block the rookie. And the kid hit Jerry, who weighed three hundred pounds. Boom! They both hit like that and went right down. Jerry dislocated his shoulder and was out for the year. I knew one thing after that, I wasn't wedge material. It didn't agree with my way.

I got off it eventually but in one early game against Philadelphia I was back to kick off and one of the Eagle linemen, Menil Mavraides, who had played for Notre Dame, started hollering, "Protect yourself, protect yourself!"

At first I couldn't understand what he meant, but I did soon enough. As soon as I kicked off he came up and I got by him, then I saw five or six other guys coming after me. Luckily, they were coming forward and I got in between them. They actually turned around and ran after me. They were all after me and I just headed for the sidelines. They just wanted to give me a little initiation, welcome me to the league.

But I got along fine with my own guys. They started giving me nicknames right away. They'd call me "Heisman," and "Plum," because I was a bonus pick, and "Golden Dome" and "Number One." I'd go out and catch a pass and they'd holler, "Atta go, Heisman."

Stevens Point is a small town and there wasn't much to do. We played a little cards at night. And I'd go out and have a few beers with Tom Bettis and Howie Ferguson. Ferguson was a real character and I got along with Fergie right away.

Then we went to Miami for our first exhibition game, and my stripper friend from Chicago was working there, and I fixed up some of the boys with some of her friends. It was funny, a rookie fixing up the veterans. But I had been to a lot of cities and made a few contacts, where they hadn't.

One of the guys came up to me in Miami and said, "How come you, a rookie, got all the tomatoes in town? First thing happened, a couple of tomatoes were waiting for you at the hotel and—pshew—there you go." What could I tell him?

Coach Blackbourn had his eye on me in Miami. I don't think he minded so much seeing me with "tomatoes." But once he caught me whispering to a Packer veteran who had quite a reputation as a lover. And Blackbourn made the comment: "Well, I knew those two would get together before long."

I had a good game against the Cardinals in Miami. I played maybe ten minutes and I threw the ball pretty well to Ron. He caught about four or five short passes. I got off a few good runs, too. And I felt elated after the ball game.

But the exhibition game I remember most was in Boston. Naturally, the write-ups that summer anywhere we went were mostly about me, Hornung with the Packers. So they decided to start me against the Giants in Boston. I played the first half and we never got past our own twenty-five-yard line. I'd try a couple of running plays and then punt, and that's all it was. I just couldn't move the club and when I tried to pass I got stormed. We were behind 6-0 at half-time and Bart Starr played the second half, and we won, 14-6.

The papers the next day were beautiful. They really tore me apart. "Fluke," they said. "Here's your bonus plum, your All-America. You can keep your Heisman Trophy winner."

But we never lost a pre-season exhibition game and we won our opener against the Chicago Bears, and everything looked great. And then we started losing, and losing, and losing.

Lisle Blackbourn was in a tough position. He had been head coach since 1954 and the Packers had gone nowhere. They were 4–8 in '54, 6–6 in '55, and 4–8 again in '56. A lot of his problems were organizational. The Packers are publicly owned, and run by a board of directors, and in those days they acted like coaches. They second-guessed everything he did and actually met with him once a week to go over mistakes made that Sunday. Everybody was a honcho in Green Bay. The board of directors were trying to run the coaches, the radio stations were trying to run the coaches, the man in the street was raising hell with the radio stations. It was a real vicious circle.

On top of that, Blackbourn didn't know what to do with me. He knew he had to play me somewhere because I was a bonus choice and the Packer fans kind of expected a lot from me. With all the publicity I had gotten from Notre Dame, the people in Green Bay figured I was gonna take Green Bay right away to the championship. So he was in a spot.

But he didn't know where to play me. He didn't want to start me at quarterback. He had Babe Parilli and Bart Starr and I think he knew then I wasn't going to make it as a quarterback. He knew very definitely that I was a good athlete and ballplayer. The question was where to put me.

So I ended up playing three positions—quarterback, halfback, fullback. And I didn't enjoy it even when I was playing quarterback. Usually, he would put me in at quarterback on third-down situations. You know, third and one, I'd go in. Fourth and a half foot, I'd go in either to run the option or quarterback sneak. And everybody would know it. One game against the Bears when I went in on that kind of situation, the Bear middle linebacker, Bill George, hollered out, "Option right, option left, roll out right, roll out left." It was kind of evident what I was going to do.

I never knew one week to the next where I was going to play. I'd find out on Sunday morning. Coach would say, "You'll play a little halfback today," or, "You'll play a little quarterback."

This went on for a while and then I realized that I didn't have the one thing to make a professional quarterback, and that's talent. It was as simple as that. I still thought I could play football, but I didn't think I actually could be a top-flight quarterback. I couldn't throw the ball accurately enough.

That's one thing about the transition from college ball to pro ball. Maybe if I had stayed with it, I could have become a quarterback. I think the prime years as far as football is concerned are twenty-six, twenty-seven, twenty-eight. You're older, you're performing better, and you do a lot of things better and more efficiently. A quarterback will throw a ball a heck of a lot better when he is twenty-seven than when he is twenty-one, and he has a lot better receivers playing with him than he had in college.

This transition from college to pros is no joke. It was bad enough in college when you were a sophomore and there was a three-year age gap between you and the seniors. But as a pro there is maybe a six- or seven-year gap. This is a very, very distinctive gap. And now you're playing with the best college players, molded into a team. You're playing with guys who hit harder, too, hit harder because they're much bigger and stronger. I don't think the rate of speed of one body hitting another is any different than college, but I think the pros know how to hit you maybe a little better.

That first game against the Chicago Bears was a high-water mark for the team, but not for me. We played in Green Bay, dedicating the new City Stadium. We beat the Bears, 21–17. I ran the ball twice—and lost ten yards. And that's all I did. Parilli and Starr were the passers. Howie Ferguson was the fullback and Fred Cone was doing the place-kicking.

My best game of the year came the following week against the Giants. I carried sixteen times, gained 112 yards. And in that game I got the Packers' longest run from scrimmage for the year, seventy-two yards. My weight was up to 230 because of my inactivity, and Em Tunnell hauled me down from behind.

I ran pretty well the next two games and then we played Pittsburgh and on my second carry, I went up the middle and broke through a nice hole. Then one of the Steelers lunged at me, grabbed my ankle from behind when he rolled, and jerked it. I sprained it and was pretty much through for the season. All in all I picked up 319 yards in sixty attempts, scored eighteen points, caught six passes. That would have been considered a good year on a winning ball club. But with my reputation, and coming to Green Bay with a losing ball club, they expected more.

Then I had more trouble with the Coach.

Despite my bad ankle I made the trip with the team to the West Coast. We were playing in San Francisco first and we stayed at the Sonora Mission Inn. I wasn't practicing and I couldn't play, my ankle was so bad. I knew I wasn't going to play and I got restless. It was just too much hanging around and playing ping-pong for three straight days. So after a few days, I snuck out and drove all over San Francisco. I met a little fiancée and we went into town a couple of nights.

The next week we went down to L.A. and I fell in love with some pretty little thing. Again I knew I wasn't going to play so I went out one night and came in the next morning about eight o'clock, in time for breakfast.

I was seen coming in the hotel in my suit and tie and it was a dead giveaway. Lisle Blackbourn called me in. He said, "One more escapade like that and I'll fine you your salary even if you're not going to play."

For the game that Sunday we were really banged up. Ron was hurt; Ferguson was hurt; Sam Palumbo, our center, had hurt his ankle and was limping around for two weeks. He kept telling the trainer that it hurt him so bad. He finally had an X-ray in California and they found out he had a broken ankle—after playing a couple of weeks on it. We had twenty-three ballplayers available out of thirty-two or thirty-three, and all the cripples sat on the bench together.

That was the only time in my life that I ever took a Benny, the pep pills that some ballplayers take. I have seen some of the players take eight or nine of them before a game. I thought I might get stuck in there so that I better take a couple. They never affected me at all. And I have never taken one since. I never needed them. I've got a lot of natural energy, you know.

I was sitting there on the bench, all suited up, and we were getting killed, and all of a sudden we were on our first offensive move. The ball was on their fifteen-yard line and we had moved about sixty yards. The score was 32–0 and it was the third quarter. I was sitting there and, all of a sudden, I heard this female voice calling, "Paul, Paul."

The game was at the Los Angeles Coliseum and the seats are about twenty yards from the bench, and you can hear the crowd pretty good. But I still wasn't sure I was hearing right.

I turned around and there was this gorgeous brunette. She said, "I want to take a picture with you."

I said, "Wait till after the game."

"No, right now."

Ferguson, sitting beside me, was laughing and the coach was down there and I'm worried he will see us. And I whispered to her, "After the game! After the game!" And Ferguson kept saying, "She is beautiful." And I said, "I don't care how beautiful she is. If Coach catches me, he'll fine me my salary. He told me last week he wanted no more shenanigans."

All of a sudden Ferguson elbowed me and said, "Guess what?"

"What?"

"She's walking over here."

"You're kidding." It couldn't be possible, I thought, not right in the middle of the game. Then I felt a light tap on my shoulder, an unmistakable feminine tap.

She whispered right in my ear, in a husky voice, "I'm not leaving until I get a picture." And she had a photographer with her.

I said, "You're kidding."

Ferguson said, "Get the hell up and take the picture. She's not going to leave—you've got to get her out of here." He was really worried now.

She repeated, "I'm not leaving until you get me a picture." I jumped up, got behind the bench. While the game was going on, while we're driving for a score, I've got my arm around a girl, in my football uniform, and the guy snapped the picture.

I said, "Get out of here, meet me at the locker room entrance after the game. I want to talk to you."

She started to walk away just as we scored. Blackbourn turned around, started to walk back down the bench, and kind of looked up and saw this girl and the photographer walking away. I don't think he knows to this day that I took a picture with the girl. But he saw me turning around and sitting down and he kind of puts two and two together.

"Hornung," he hollered. "Go in there and kick off." It was my right ankle that was hurt but I went out there. I wasn't going to say, "Hell, no, I can't kick off." I knew I couldn't kick off but I figure I had to go out there.

So I went out and kicked the ball, about five yards—beautiful. It went poof-poof-poof, and Duane Putnam, who weighed 250 pounds, came up and hit me and turned me for about two somersaults. With my bad ankle I couldn't get out of the way, and I came off that field with tears in my eyes, glassy-eyed. He almost killed me.

There is a sad epilogue to that story. I did see the girl

after the ball game, and I did get her number and then I lost the damn thing.

We ended up in 1957 with a 3–9 record and it certainly wasn't all Blackbourn's fault. He was a good coach but I don't think he handled the guys right. He let them develop a don't-give-a-damn attitude. Halfway through the season they were out of it—they didn't care. And it's just terrible playing for a team like that. It's no fun. You want to go out on the field, you want to win. These guys were just putting in time. They didn't care and I did care, I cared a hell of a lot.

Right after the season, Lisle Blackbourn was fired and I went into the United States Army.

2. THEY CALL ME "PICCADILLY PAUL"

At least I didn't have time to brood over what had happened to me in 1957, which I wouldn't have done anyway, since I'm not a brooder. I was in the Army Reserve and I was called up for my six months' active service. It was a beautiful time in the service. I did basic training and I was in the best shape of my life. Sherrill Sipes and I went in together and Steve Myhra of the Baltimore Colts was there, and Joe Walton, who was playing with the Washington Redskins then. And we were stationed at Fort Knox, Kentucky, which is only twenty-eight miles from Louisville. We'd go in town every weekend and, after basic, almost every night.

I was a clerk-typist and after clerk-typist I was a softball coach. I also had charge of cutting the grass in my company. We had two big power lawnmowers and I had four assistants, and the logistics problem was this: I had to plan every day what part of the grass to cut.

Then we formed a basketball team to compete in the camp championship. We had a colonel who was the head of our battalion and he was gung-ho, he really wanted to win. I did, too. I don't remember ever wanting to win anything so hard in my life. Because if we won we got a four-day pass and we wouldn't have to go on bivouac. We had Sipes and myself and a kid from a small school in Kentucky and we practiced every day and every night.

I never will forget this sergeant in Sipes' platoon who was just dying to get me. Actually he was a great guy but he was a big, loud, tough type of sergeant. He was waiting till I did something wrong, you know, so that he could get me down and give me fifty push-ups. But I was playing basketball and that frustrated him. He came up to me one day and said, "How come you play basketball so good? I thought you were a football player."

He didn't like it because maybe we'd walk a few miles out to a detail and by the time we got there at ten o'clock the truck would come around for the basketball team. They'd say, okay, the basketball team fall out. And we'd get back in the truck and practice all afternoon. Well, the sergeant just hated that.

We must have played thirty-five games, we played three times a week, and we got in the tournament, and we won the post championship.

So we came back off leave on Monday and we discovered there was still five days of bivouac left, five days of life in a sleeping bag. We had to figure out something. So that night the colonel came down and announced that there was a volleyball tournament coming up. "We have to have a volleyball team in it," he said. "Any of you men ever play volleyball?"

I had never played volleyball in my life but my hand shot up. "Hell, yes, I played volleyball!" I said. Well, we went out to the bivouac area and the sergeant saw us and his eyes lit up. "Ah, Sipes and Hornung, our long, lost jockstraps." Then he exploded. "Give me twenty!" And we fell down and started doing push-ups. Just then a truck roared up, screeched to a halt, the driver got out and yelled, "Volleyball team, fall out!"

So Sipes and I picked ourselves up and we climbed into the truck. The sergeant looked stricken. His face had fallen to his navel. "Wait a minute," he said, "you don't play volleyball too, do you?"

I said, "Yes, sir. I play volleyball." Oh, he was dying. He was crushed.

So we played volleyball for three days. We didn't win a ball game but we couldn't afford to be out of that tournament.

Later I played on the softball team. I was a pitcher, Joe Walton was the center fielder, Sipes was the catcher. We had a pretty good fast-pitch team. I wasn't that good a pitcher but I was a little fast and after I hit about four or five, they'd be scared to death to come up.

It was a helluva way to spend the off-season and when I reported to the Packers in the summer of '58, I was in real great shape and raring to go.

I had hopes that things would be different in Green Bay. Ray "Scooter" McLean, who was our backfield coach in '57, was the new head coach, and we all loved the guy. But it just didn't work out.

First of all, the fact that everybody loved Scooter was bad. You have to have a certain amount of discipline and respect in a coach, and distance between the coach and his players. But Scooter was like a friend, like one of the guys. He played in our poker games and he had no curfew and put the team on its honor, which was probably his biggest mistake.

Another thing, he kept Lisle Blackbourn's system and elaborated on it and it was a bad system. For instance, we would have different offensive blocking on every play. And then we'd change back and forth from week to week. It got so the guys would be pulling and hitting each other and going the wrong way and missing the blocks. It was just too difficult. Everybody was getting all screwed up.

It was bad personally, too. Until the seventh game of the season, I never got to carry the ball more than five times in any one game. Like Blackbourn, McLean didn't know where to play me. I played some halfback, but mostly fullback, behind Howie Ferguson, and we were losing every game and I was getting a little disgusted, and maybe that's why I kind of started running around more than I should have.

Actually, I wasn't too happy about Green Bay in those days.

The first time I visited Green Bay was in May of 1957 and I froze, it was so cold. But I got a good impression of the town. The people were very nice when I came up. I made an appearance at a show and I went back during the summer and they had an affair for us at the Notre Dame Club.

In my first season I shared a house with Max McGee and Billy Howton and, looking back, that was quite a thing, a rookie living with a couple of veterans. Naturally, being a bachelor, I wasn't going to hang around watching *The Untouchables* every night. We had our favorite watering spots in town. Speed's bar was one, the Lyric Lounge was another, the Piccadilly was a third. I liked to go out and unwind and naturally I liked to date, and there is *nowhere* to hide in Green Bay. Baby, you are out in the open. Green Bay is such a small town that everyone knows the color of your underwear. You could be sitting at the bar drinking Seven-Up and the next day it would have been champagne.

The trouble of course was that we were losing, and when you lose, you're supposed to be off in a corner hiding, not running around in public. And because we were losing, rumors spread, and some of the rumors were true. Everybody can't go through seven months by living at home, or staying in all the time. I learned after we started winning

that Green Bay is a real great sports town, full of nice people. And even when we were losing there was only a small
percentage in town who felt that if we lost we should stay
home and not go out. It's okay if Green Bay wins—fine. The
boys should be out tonight having a beer. But if you lose, you
better not come out tonight, you better stay in a cage somewhere. And this small percentage are really the trouble-
makers or rumor-spreaders. And in a small town, they can
do a great deal of damage.

So I didn't like the town at first. I said the hell with it. I
was going to do what I wanted. That was the train of
thought. But you just can't do that in a small town when
you're in the public eye. It's as simple as that.

And the rumors about Paul Hornung, about "Piccadilly
Paul" as some people chose to call me in those days, were
abundant. There was one beaut. Bobby Layne and I were
picked up stoned at five-thirty one morning in some doorway downtown. I didn't know Bobby then and if I did, you
can bet your life we wouldn't have been picked up in a
doorway.

Later there was a rumor that Max McGee and I had
wrecked our car, that Max had run the car off the road at
five on the morning of a game. Well, naturally, we were at
home all the time, fast asleep.

Some rumors of course had certain bases in fact. One
Sunday night in 1958 after we had played the Bears—and
had been beaten—a bunch of us all went out to dinner. Billy
Howton, Bill Forester, Al Carmichael were with their wives;
Max and I had dates.

After dinner we went to the Piccadilly and we had a few
drinks and were feeling pretty good. They had a swinging
combo there and Max and I went up on the bandstand to
sing. We sang a couple of songs and then I went back up

and did a solo. I sang, "Won't You Come Home, Bill Bailey," or something like that.

And it was hot and crowded and we had been dancing, and I loosened my tie, took off my coat, and unbuttoned my shirt. Howton was up on the bandstand playing the piano, Bill Forester was playing the drums, and I was singing this song, with my coat off and shirt unbuttoned.

And, actually, I was the first one to get up and leave with my date.

Well, the next day the news had spread all over town that Paul Hornung had done a strip at the Piccadilly. They even had reports that my girl had confirmed it. Somebody said they had talked to her and she had said, "Yes, he did a strip."

I was so damned mad. I went right back to see her. "How in the world could you say that, honey," I said. "You know I didn't leave you till three or four in the morning."

She said, "Well, I thought you went back after you left me."

I said, "Well, you big dummy, you know the place closes at one or two o'clock. Do you think they kept it open for me?"

It was ridiculous but there it was. Piccadilly Paul rides again.

So there were a few little incidents like that, blown out of all proportion. Never anything worse. I did get in one fight in Green Bay, but that was in 1962 and was just a bad mistake on my part.

It was a Sunday night and I was coming out of Jesse Whittenton's restaurant. I had had a few martinis and I had a date and it was very cold and two guys walked out at the same time.

One of them said, "Well, Golden Boy might not be playing any more but he can still get the women."

I said, "Pardon me?" I was in a bad mood, anyway. I had

been out three weeks with a bad knee and I didn't feel
worth a damn because I hadn't been playing, and you never
feel good when you're not playing. "Wait one second," I
said.

He walked up to me. I put my championship ring on my
right hand and when he got close he started to say something and I just swung. And I hit him, which was wrong—
flat, double wrong. I could either have had a lawsuit on my
hands or I could get the hell kicked out of me—one or the
two.

We wrestled each other to the ground and now the guy's
friend piles on. I had this heavy overcoat on and it was cold
and I couldn't do a thing. They were half stoned or I guess
they really could have done a job on me.

Well, someone told Jesse that there was a difference of
opinion going on outside, and he ran right out and separated
everybody. We talked it over and everything was patched
up. It was a very stupid thing for me to do and I regret it to
this day.

But that was my only altercation in Green Bay and the
rest was exaggerated out of all proportion because we were
losers.

We sure were losers in 1958. We won one game and tied
one, and that was all. But I began to play a little more from
the seventh game on. Against the Rams in Green Bay, I carried eleven times for sixty-three yards. The next Sunday I
got ninety-two yards in twelve carries. In Detroit on Thanksgiving day I made fifty yards in eight carries. Then, on the
West Coast, I sat out two games. Scooter put in the rookie
fullback, Jim Taylor, who had finally figured out the complicated McLean offense. Jim had two very strong games
against San Francisco and the Rams.

That Ram game was the last one and my statistics didn't
look too bad considering the season we had had. I led the

club in rushing, with 310 yards in sixty-nine carries (a 4.5 average), and in scoring with sixty-seven points. I kicked eleven out of twenty-one field goals, twenty-two extra points, and scored two touchdowns.

But I went back to Louisville in a very low mood, thinking that if I didn't get traded, maybe I ought to quit.

For one thing, getting switched from position to position was just no good. It was very tiring mentally for me. For another, I hated losing. Some people in Green Bay, taking note of my extracurricular activities, said that Hornung had an I-don't-care attitude. But I did care. I cared so much that I wanted to get out of there and play somewhere else. I was twenty-three years old and I still wanted to prove to myself that I could play professional football.

We had such a messed-up situation it was unbelievable. There were guys who were just playing individually, playing for the money, for next year's contract. They were the ones who didn't care. And there were others who weren't playing and wanted to and yet couldn't, and, as a result, they didn't know what they were doing. And I was one of them. It was just a bad situation all around and naturally, when you're around it, some of it has to rub off on you.

And, naturally, you want to be with a winning team. I think it's everybody's feeling. Living in the National Football League when you're a loser is like operating a business in the red. You're not too happy and your whole personality changes.

So I went back to Louisville and Mom, who was real concerned, said, "Do you really want to quit, Paul?"

And I said, "No, of course not, Mom. I might have told a writer that if this keeps up, it's ridiculous. But I'm not quitting. I'll try it another year."

I still hoped to find out what it was like winning in the National Football League.

3. BEHOLD, THE MESSIAH

Right after the '58 season, Scooter McLean beat everyone to the punch by announcing his resignation as head coach of the Packers. It was accepted unanimously and I think Ray was glad to get out of there.

The situation in Green Bay had gone from worse to worser. For eleven straight seasons, the Packers had been losers (thirty-seven wins against ninety-three losses) and any coach that took the job had to be crazy. It was like going up as a pinch-hitter against Sandy Koufax with a two-strike count. The chief trouble was organizational. As I have said, everyone in Green Bay was getting into the act. The coach had to answer to a board of thirteen directors, the board had to answer to radio, television, and newspapers, the press had to answer to the fans. Everyone was second-guessing everyone else. What Green Bay needed at this time was a dictator, one man who would be in charge all by himself, a messiah who could lead his stray flock to the Promised Land.

One of that stray flock wandered back to Louisville and did some work in real estate, and tried to pull himself together. I went up to Cincinnati one night for a banquet at the same time that the N.F.L. Coaches' Association was in town for a meeting. I saw Jack Vainisi, our harried business manager, and asked Jack if he had gotten a coach yet. He said no. "We've got about twenty applicants," Jack said, shaking his head, "don't ask me why."

I heard a number of names mentioned for the job when I was in Cincinnati. One was Vince Lombardi. Then I went back home and, soon after, Vincent Thomas Lombardi, offensive coach of the New York Giants, was named coach and general manager—with total control of the team. If that were true, then things had to get better.

The day the announcement was made, Mom came home and said, "Do you know anything about him?"

"Not much," I said, "but I know he's got a good reputation."

And he had. Vince Lombardi had been a successful football player at Fordham, one of their famous "Seven Blocks of Granite." He had been a successful high school coach, a successful assistant to Red Blaik at Army, and then a very successful offense coach with the New York Giants for five years. He seemed to have the credentials, all right.

Soon after he took over I got a phone call from Coach Lombardi. He just said he was looking forward to meeting me. Then he sent me a couple of letters. The message was clear: "We certainly want you to be in good shape," he wrote. "In fact, you better be in the best physical shape of your life. That training camp's going to be tough."

You could tell from those letters that he was his own man, and that he was very serious-minded. An Army type, I thought, and that's just what we need.

One day in June Mom was reading the Green Bay *Press-Gazette* that featured an interview with Lombardi. Lombardi was quoted as telling the writer, Art Daley, "Let's face it. Hornung is the guy who can make us go. He's a key player and much of our success will depend on him. We'll see what he can do as a pass-run option halfback. We know he can run and pass, but how much will depend on how quick he is, and how quickly he can decide whether to run or pass."

Mom finished the article and she was beaming. "Well," she said, "looks like you've got a definite job. You're the left halfback."

I said, "That sounds good. We ought to go out to dinner tonight and celebrate." And that's what we did.

In T-formation football, the quarterback is naturally the key man, but in the Lombardi concept the left halfback is very important, too. With the Giants, Lombardi's big man was Frank Gifford, the left halfback. Giff functioned almost as a single-wing tailback in the way he had to make his cut over tackle, behind double-pull blocking, and in his exercise of the option pass-run, which puts the big burden on the defense to commit itself. The halfback also has to show adaptability to dive through on quick openers, to block, to decoy, to catch passes, and to take a beating.

That was the job Coach had in mind for me in Green Bay, and I could hardly wait.

I met him for the first time when I drove to St. Norbert's College for the opening of practice. I arrived that day just in time for the six o'clock meal, and he walked up to me in the chow hall. "I'm Coach Lombardi," he said, extending his hand, "nice to have you here, Paul."

He didn't look any way I had pictured him. He didn't look coach-like. He wore glasses and he had this gentle kind of smile and he looked almost like a college professor; except that he was stocky and built tough and you could almost smell the toughness under that mild exterior.

Naturally, everyone was wondering how he was and we found out right away, at our first meeting.

The first thing he did, he started talking about winning. "I've never been a losing coach," he said, "and I don't intend to start here." He spoke slowly, easily, in a deep, gruff voice that sounded like authority itself, a voice that meant business.

He continued. "There is nobody big enough to think he's got the team made or can do what he wants. Trains and planes are going in and coming out of Green Bay every day, and he'll be on one of them. I won't. I'm going to find thirty-six men who have the pride to make any sacrifice to win. There are such men. If they're not here, I'll get them. If you are not one, if you don't want to play, you might as well leave right now."

Then he started talking about rules and regulations.

"I've been up here all year," he said, "and I've learned a lot. I know how the townspeople are and what they think of you men and I know that in a small town you need definite rules and regulations. And anybody who breaks the rules will be taken care of in my own way."

So he set curfews. Curfew at St. Norbert's was 11 P.M. One night Em Tunnell, one of our defensive backs, arrived five minutes late. Coach was waiting for him at the door.

"That will be fifty dollars," he said. We all heard about that.

He also set certain places in town off-limits. He put the Piccadilly off-limits and two other places downtown, only because they were near the main hotel. He said he knew everybody liked to have a few beers, a few drinks, but he didn't want his players to be seen drinking right next to the hotel, where there were so many salesmen coming in from out of town.

He held a private meeting with me, too.

"I know about your reputation here," he said. "I've investigated you very carefully. You have done things you shouldn't have done, but I don't think you've done as many things as people say you've done."

I looked him right in the eye. "If that's the way they want to think, that's the way they'll think."

He grinned. "I trust you, and don't forget that. I just don't want you to let me down. If you do, it'll be your ———." I got the message.

He handled himself real well, you could see that right away. He was a man not only of football intelligence but good common sense. Just a man of strength. You could also see he was the boss. From the very first practice, there was no more of the board of directors and people all hanging around and doing this and doing that and telling the coaches what to do. You could see that he was general manager and head coach and he was going to run the show the way he saw fit.

That first day of practice, he put it right to me. Before we got started he came up to me, took me by the arm, and said, "Well, you're going to be my left halfback. You're either going to play left halfback or you're not going to play. How do you feel about that?"

"I'm glad," I said. I was, too. I wanted to play one position instead of three. I welcomed the opportunity. Naturally I knew how he ran the offense in New York and how Gifford had been very, very successful there. And if I was going to be given a chance at left halfback in the same system, I thought that was very good.

I really wanted to play football that fall and, after a few practices, I felt for the first time that I was getting something out of football. Coach Lombardi's system was fabulous. There was a meaning for everything we did. His system would dictate why you did something in a given situation—why, for instance, you would block the end with your right shoulder against a particular defense. In the past, you would do something and that would be it. You wouldn't know why, or the reason behind it. The coach would just say, this is the way the play was drawn up. But with Lombardi, everything had a reason behind it, everything he did. And he explained it to the ballplayers that way. And naturally we began to play football.

Emphasis in the training camp was on conditioning, timing, agility, and reaction. We had workouts that lasted maybe one hour and fifteen minutes, shorter than we had had under Blackbourn or McLean. But they were so concentrated that there was never a second wasted. We had wind sprints (twenty-yard dashes at full speed), one-on-one blocking, and tackling practice, and lots of movies. We watched movies till the whole world looked like Cinerama. Lombardi had movies broken down to everything—to blocking, individual tackling, particular plays. I remember one day one of the guys came in from a date and I said, "How'd you make out?"

"I don't know," he said. "I'll have to see the movies."

Coach also made some trades to strengthen us. He got Bill Quinlan, Henry Jordan, and Willie Davis from Cleveland. He got Lew Carpenter from Detroit. He brought in Fuzzy Thurston, who had kicked around with four other teams. He got rid of some guys he felt didn't fit in with his system.

That system was essentially ball control. We started off with the three-back system, three running backs rather than two running backs and a flanker that every pro team plays today. Sometimes we'd keep the three backs and run from a full T. Other times one of the backs would flank one way or another.

The No. 1 play in Coach Lombardi's system was the offense sweep, both guards out in front of the halfback. The other big play for me was the option.

The option of course is taken off the end run sweep. The blocking is the same as the end run sweep and the object is that it's supposed to look like the sweep. The reason the option is there is because if all the potential receivers are covered, then it does become an end sweep. The tight end blocks the linebacker for three counts, just as he does on end sweeps, and the only difference is that he releases. And the flanker is already downfield as he is in the end sweep, and you have your guards pulling and the fullback is blocking the end the same way as the end sweep. So if everybody is covered you just holler—go—you know. And if they're not covered, naturally you're just going to throw a pass.

And I had to learn that when I wasn't carrying the ball, I had to hit somebody. I'd have to block the defensive end or a linebacker. Very seldom wasn't I hitting anyone, except when I was running a faking pattern. Otherwise, you were hitting somebody at all times. Coach's philosophy of offense was direct: Try to knock everybody down on every play.

We started the exhibition season with Lamar McHan the quarterback, Jimmy Taylor the fullback, Don McIlhenny the right halfback, me at left half.

We lost our first exhibition game against Pittsburgh in the mud, 6–3. I remember that one because it's the only game I've ever played in that I felt should have been called off. You couldn't tell where the field was. It was raining so hard you couldn't see thirty yards downfield.

Then we won all but one of our other exhibition games.

Coach has a definite feeling about exhibition games. He wants to win everything, you know, everytime he steps on the field. The other coaches, naturally, they want to win, but they don't want to kill themselves during the exhibition season.

I had some good exhibition games; there were a couple of games when I scored all the points and I was kicking, too, so I was quite happy.

We opened the season against the Chicago Bears and we beat them, 9–6. Jimmy rushed for ninety-eight yards, I rushed for sixty-one. On the option I completed my second pass as a pro, a twenty-yarder, then I hit on another one.

We beat Detroit 28–10 in the second game and I picked up forty-five yards rushing, and kicked four extra points.

Then the San Francisco 49ers came in to Green Bay and my Mom and Uncle Henry were both up for the game, and it was my best game to date as a pro.

I had to do the heavy-duty work because Jimmy Taylor, during the week, had burned himself severely at home when grease in a frying pan caught fire. He was to miss the next three games. Lew Carpenter moved to fullback. I carried twenty-eight times in that game. I gained 138 yards, including an eight-yard touchdown run. The third touchdown came in the third quarter and I kicked my third straight extra point and that was it; we beat the 49ers 21–20.

I was supposed to take Mom and Uncle Henry to dinner after the game, but I was really dead. Leo Nomellini, the 49ers' defensive tackle, had done a job on me. He had been in on every play. So instead of dinner, I checked into St. Vincent's Hospital for a rest.

Then the bubble burst. We lost our next five games in a row. Naturally, Jimmy being out hurt us quite a bit. We had been controlling the football; that was our game. With him out of there, it hurt our control game.

Los Angeles killed us, 45–6. I kicked two field goals, gained fifty-four yards rushing, caught five passes, but that was a deluge; everything broke loose. Then Baltimore beat us 38–21 and that was one of my worst games. (My worst was against the Bears that year when I fumbled the ball four times; I never fumble the ball more than twice a year.) Then we went to New York and the Giants licked us 20–3 and there was one unique play in that game.

It was late in the last period and Joe Francis was the quarterback. We were still using the three-back system and when the flanker was to the left, I'd be that flanker. When I went out to the flank, the Giants' defensive back, Dick Lynch, who had played with me at Notre Dame, hollered, "What are you going to do, Hornung?"

"Down and in," I said. Well, the play was called in the huddle and it was a play on the right side. But Francis changed the call at the line of scrimmage and now the pass pattern was on the left side—which was me, going down and cutting in the middle.

I went down, cut in, Francis hit me in the belly, and Lynch came up and made the tackle. On the ground he growled, "I'll be damned, you sonofagun, you weren't kidding me."

One thing that surprised us through that losing streak was how Coach handled us. He was such a tough, stern man, that we expected him to really chew us out. Naturally, he was peeved at losing those games but he treated everybody with a lot of respect. He told us, if you give 100 per cent, if you block and tackle and do not make mental mistakes, if you give everything you can give and if you still lose under those circumstances, you just have to accept it. It seemed that sometimes he was a lot easier to live with when he was losing.

And we kept losing. The Bears beat us 28–17 and then we met Baltimore again, and that game was kind of a turning point in the fortunes of the Green Bay Packers.

We started off like we had in the previous four games— lousy. At halftime we were down 20–3, and it was then that Coach made some key changes. He decided to play Bart Starr at quarterback. He scrapped his three-back system and moved rookie Boyd Dowler into flanker. Dowler caught eight passes that second half, we all picked up, and almost beat Baltimore. The final score was 28–24. I averaged nearly ten yards a carry in eight rushes, kicked three extra points, and kicked a twenty-three-yard field goal.

Up to then, though, I had been no sensation. I had scored only one touchdown, kicked sixteen extra points and five field goals, a total of thirty-seven points. Jimmy, who had missed three games, was only seven points behind me.

With Jimmy healthy again and Bart coming into his own, and our defense jelling, we began to move. Bart completed eleven of nineteen passes against Washington and we beat them, 21–0. I scored a touchdown, kicked a field goal, and gained eighty-one yards rushing.

On Thanksgiving Day before a national television audience, our rating went way up. We beat the Lions, 24–17. I scored two touchdowns, three extra points, and a field goal. The touchdowns both came on tough off-tackle plays. Both times I had linebackers come up to meet me, both times I was able to hip fake, cut, and use a little power. My running technique is a bit different than a Jimmy Brown or Jim Taylor. I don't shed tackles like Brown and Taylor shed tackles. They break tackles so effortlessly you'd think the guy just missed the tackle. With Taylor it's hit a lot of times right on through them, or back up and come at 'em again real quick. With Brown, it's just right on through. With me it's more like hit, and then a little go. I just hit and try to find an open hole.

The next week on the Coast I had a big game against Los Angeles. We all did, in fact. Jimmy scored two touchdowns, Bart completed eleven of twenty passes. I picked up seventy-four yards rushing and threw two touchdown passes on the option, one for twenty-six yards, one for thirty. We won 38–20 and now I had seventy-two points for the season, with one game left. Pat Summerall of the Giants was leading the league in scoring with eighty-six points,

fourteen ahead of me. And I was thinking, wouldn't I love
to catch him.

We went into San Francisco to play the 49ers and it was
a lovely way to end a season.

Bart had a tremendous day with twenty out of twenty-five
completions for 249 yards. And I scored twenty-two points.
I scored three touchdowns on runs of thirteen, three, and
two yards. I kicked four extra points. We beat San Francisco 36–14, which enabled us to tie the 49ers for third
place in the Western Conference. My total for the season
was ninety-four points. Pat Summerall finished with ninety,
and I had won my first scoring title. The only thing that
went wrong in that game was that I missed the last extra
point, the last one I was to miss until 1964.

Naturally, everyone was very happy. After the game,
Coach came around and congratulated us and passed out
Pro Bowl selections and I had made the Pro Bowl team for
the first time. I had had a better year than both of the previous two combined. I ran more times in 1959 than I had in
1957 or '58 (152 to 129). I gained more yardage (681 to
619), completed more passes (five to one), gained more
yardage passing (95 to minus one), scored more touchdowns (seven to five), and more points (94 to 85). And I
led the club in rushing attempts, rushing yardage, scoring,
and passing.

Now I felt I was a pro. Now I felt I belonged, and Vince
Lombardi was the man responsible. If it hadn't been for
him, we probably would have still been nowhere. I told a
writer after that last game, "If Lombardi told me to move
out wide on the next play, jump over the wall, land in the
stands, and buy a program, I think I would have done it."

4. MY GREATEST YEAR

So I signed a new three-year contract for twenty-one thousand dollars a year, plus bonuses for scoring, and told a sportswriter that would be my last three years in professional football.

That's the way I felt at the time. When I went into pro ball, I figured if I could play six years, that would be more than the average. And I felt I wanted to get definitely set in business somewhere and I knew that playing in a big city you do get set up, and I wanted security. There weren't many good job opportunities in Green Bay. I didn't know what I was going to do. I just didn't want to play nine or ten years and end up with no job and having to start all over again. If I had to do that, I wouldn't play. I was not yet twenty-five and I felt I had better start thinking of my future.

Besides, when I made that statement about quitting after three more years, I was in a bad mood. Back home I had lost my driver's license. They have the point system in Kentucky and after the '59 season I got a couple of quick speeding tickets and that gave me too many points and they took away my license. I think it was the worst six months I ever had in my life, being without a car. It cramped my style, naturally.

Then I went back up to St. Norbert's for pre-season camp and that was the summer Max and I got caught out after curfew.

What happened was that we had met a couple of girls and made a date to meet them one night after midnight. Curfew at St. Norbert's is about 11 P.M., so it was about one in the morning and Max slipped out of bed, put on his clogs, and walked down the corridor to the pay phone. The only thing was, a couple of the assistant coaches and a sportswriter were still in the office, jawing. They heard Max clattering down the hall and he had to think fast.

"Need a drink of water," he said.

Later I found out what had happened. Max went into the phone booth to make the call and he was seen. The sportswriter said, "Max has just put a nickel in the water cooler."

He set up the dates, came back to our room, which was on the first floor, we both got dressed and went out the window.

The next morning we had a message waiting for us. "Will you tell Mr. Hornung and Mr. McGee that I'd like to see them right away." That confrontation with Coach Lombardi cost us five hundred dollars apiece.

Otherwise, it was a beautiful summer. We won every pre-season exhibition game. We scored 175 points, allowed only seventy-one. The world looked good.

Then we went out and blew our season's opener with the Bears.

We had a 14–0 lead after three quarters. Jimmy had scored one touchdown, I had scored the other. Then they pulled off a couple of big plays. Willie Galimore sprinted for one touchdown, Rick Casares went for the other, and with three seconds left, they kicked a field goal, and we had lost, 17–14.

We knew we had a real good chance to win the Western

Conference title but this was a helluva way to show it. The team felt kind of down but Coach got us up quickly during the week because we had the Lions coming in, and the Lions' defense has always been our biggest problem. Any time you have a good day against Detroit, you figure it's a little bit extra, a little bit more satisfying. And that's the way it turned out. We won, 28–9. Jimmy gained 151 yards and scored a touchdown. I gained seventy-three yards rushing, and two touchdowns, one on an eleven-yard carry, the other a sixteen-yard pass reception.

The next week we played Baltimore and we didn't have a particularly good game, but we won anyway, 35–21. We had four pass interceptions and two recovered fumbles and I gained seventy-seven yards in thirteen attempts.

San Francisco came in and we were really up. We won 41–14 and I had my best game. Naturally when you have a good day you feel good and when you win it's even more so, and that's how I felt that night celebrating with the boys. I had gained seventy-two yards, scored two touchdowns, completed a pass, caught a pass, kicked two field goals including a forty-seven yarder, and five straight extra points.

Then we went in and beat Pittsburgh 19–13 and I kicked four field goals and we were in first place all by ourselves, and driving.

Next we met Baltimore for what the writers termed a "crucial" game, which it was, naturally, except that they're all crucial during a season. And we went flat. John Unitas bombed us with three straight touchdown passes and it was 21–7 at halftime. We did have a good third quarter. I scored two touchdowns and kicked a field goal and that made the score 24–24 going into the last period. Then Unitas hit again with two more touchdown passes and we were finished, 38–24. I had eighteen points. I completed one pass, caught

five for forty-seven yards, and gained ninety-nine yards on
seventeen tries, but we still lost. And we didn't feel too
good riding home on the plane that night.

Through six games I had scored eighty-three points,
which gave me a definite shot at the N.F.L. season scoring
record, set by Don Hutson in 1942. Hutson, playing for
Green Bay, had scored 138 points in eleven games. At the
end of six games he had scored eighty-two points. So I was
right with him.

But we also had a shot at the Western Conference title
and that was our goal, and mine, too. Scoring records are
fine, but we wanted the big one.

We beat Dallas 41–7 and I scored seventeen points. Then
Los Angeles came in and I picked up nineteen points and
threw a touchdown pass to Dowler, but the Rams beat us
33–31 and we dropped out of the Western Conference lead,
trailing Baltimore by a full game.

Five days later, on Thanksgiving Day, we lost to the
Lions, 23–10. I scored the ten points but their defense just
contained us. We were at Detroit's Willow Run Airport and
the Muzak was blaring, "The Party's Over," and Jim Ringo,
our center and captain, muttered, "Listen, they're playing
our song." That's the way we felt, with a 5–4 record to Baltimore's 6–2.

But it was better after Sunday's games. Baltimore lost to
San Francisco and now the standings in the West looked
like this:

Baltimore	6–3
Chicago	5–3–1
San Francisco	5–4
Green Bay	5–4

We had the Bears next in Chicago and a chance to make

those standings look a lot prettier. I had a chance, too, in this game to break Hutson's record. I had 129 points going into the Bears' game. Another ten would do it.

It started out as a defensive battle. At the end of the first period it was 0–0. Then we moved down to the Bears' twenty-one, were stopped, and I kicked a field goal. A few moments later Willie Davis blocked a punt and recovered it in the end zone. I kicked the extra point and it was 10–0.

The Bears came right back with a touchdown but missed the point. And, on the last play of the first half, I kicked a forty-one-yard field goal. We went into the dressing room ahead 13–6, and I still needed three points for that scoring record.

Tom Moore, our rookie halfback, took the kickoff to start the second half and ran the hell out of it, all the way down to the Bears' twenty. Jimmy ran three yards. Second and seven. We moved into the huddle and Bart called for a pass, with Max McGee the primary receiver. On this type of play I'm the swing back. I go out on the flat as a safety valve. If Bart's primary receiver is covered, and his secondary receivers, too, or he gets a real quick rush from the linebacker, he just dumps out real quick to one of his swing men—Jimmy or myself.

And everybody was covered deep and Bart saw that the linebacker who was supposed to be on me, Fred Williams, was off me a little bit. He just threw it out to me. I caught it and faked Fred and went in for the score without being touched. And Don Hutson's record was now mine. Then I kicked point 143 right through the uprights.

In the fourth quarter, leading comfortably, 34–13, Bart called an audible at the line of scrimmage. In fact he changed plays three times, waiting for the Bears' defense to set. I took the ball and ran ten yards for another touchdown and this was when I flipped the ball into the stands.

A legend has kind of grown up about that play. I noticed
during the 1964 season, Bucky Pope, a rookie for the Rams,
did the same thing in one of their games. Afterwards they
asked him why and he said, "Well, I understand Paul Hornung did it once."

Part of the legend, too, was that I had flipped the ball to
a girl I was dating that night. Well, that was a lot of non-
sense. If I had had a date at the game, she wouldn't have
been sitting behind the goal posts, I'll tell you that. I'm not
that cheap to put my girl in the end zone. It was just a spon-
taneous gesture. I was happy about scoring, I was happy I
had broken Hutson's record, and everybody was leaning
over the rail and screaming, "Throw the ball! Throw the
ball!" And I just flipped it up.

After the game Rick Casares came over to me and said,
"I've always wanted to do that. It was absolutely beautiful."

But George Halas, the Bears' coach, wasn't so enchanted.
He just flipped through the wall when he saw me do that.
He said, "That son of a buck, I'll send him a bill for that." So
afterwards I told Coach that he would probably be getting
a bill from Halas for throwing a $24.95 ball away. Coach
said, "Well, don't worry about it, I'll personally pay for that."

To make things even sweeter, Detroit beat Baltimore in
the last second of their game, and now we were back up
there, tied for first with Baltimore and San Francisco.

And two games to go, San Francisco and Los Angeles on
the Coast. Baltimore was on the Coast, too, playing Los
Angeles and San Francisco.

I love partying when we go to the Coast but this was one
trip I restrained myself a little. I stalled off my San Francisco fiancée; there was too much at stake. We worked out
at the Stanford University campus in Palo Alto, and Coach
wouldn't allow anybody near the field. It was like a con-
centration camp.

Actually, I wasn't sure I was going to be able to play in the 49er game. I had twisted my knee in the Bear game. It didn't bother me until Monday morning when I woke up and then it had swollen up bad. When I got to the Coast, I showed it to Dr. Nellen, our team physician, and he gave me a shot of hydrocortisone, and novocaine for the pain. I was in the locker room and he gave me the shot and he said, "How are you feeling?"

I said, "All right." I started to get up and he said, "Why don't you lay down there for a while, let it go through your system."

I said, "No, it's okay." I got up off the table and hit the floor. I passed right out.

But the shot worked just great. I didn't think I would even be trotting by Thursday but by Thursday I was running, and on Sunday I was ready.

Sunday morning in the dressing room I had the knee taped and Coach came in and talked to us. He said, "We're definitely in the running for the championship. All you have to worry about is winning your last two games. If we win our last two the worst we can do is get into a playoff. We're definitely the best team in the league," he said. "We've come this far so let's not go out and give it away."

It was raining and the field was very muddy and we had to stay on the ground. With fifty-one seconds left in the first half, I kicked a thirty-eight-yard field goal, and that was the first score of the game.

It stayed that way until late in the fourth quarter when we had the ball on the San Francisco forty-eight. Bart called for the 49 sweep, which is just our regular power sweep. I started right, our guards Jerry Kramer and Fuzzy Thurston pulled and began clearing a path. Jimmy Taylor hit the defensive end perfectly. I cut to the outside, following my blockers, Kramer and Thurston. When I got two yards from the goal line, I just dove—belly-flopped in the mud into the end zone. I was just so happy to get into the end zone that all that mud looked like gold to me.

A few moments later I kicked a field goal from the twenty-three, and all of Green Bay's thirteen points were mine. Afterwards, the boys presented me with the game ball.

The next day we watched the Baltimore-L.A. game on television and it was beautiful. The Rams won 10–3 and now we were alone in first place and all we had to do was beat the Rams and we would be champions of the Western Conference.

The Rams were fired up and scored first and took a 7–0 lead. Then Bart cranked up. He threw fifty-seven yards to Max McGee for one, then a ninety-one-yard pass-and-run play to Dowler. Then it was my turn.

We had the ball on the Rams' forty-two and Bart called for the option. I started right and saw McGee break clear, and I threw. The ball was over a little too far and Max dove for it and fell in the end zone clutching the damn ball to his bosom. It was a great catch.

And we won 35–21 and we were Western Conference champions and we went back to the hotel and had a champagne party, mostly financed on the thousand Max and I had had taken away from us for our St. Norbert caper.

Coach was very happy. He thanked us all for the great effort all year. He said he was pleased with the cooperation and effort we had given. It was a regular executive-type speech—the kind a chairman of a successful company might give if he had made ten million dollars extra that year.

He also reminded us we had one more game to go, but we weren't at that moment terribly concerned about the Eastern Conference champions, the Philadelphia Eagles. Max and I had some fiancées lined up afterwards and we got out on the Strip and tore it up a little bit.

I felt I had some celebrating coming to me. It had been my best year as a pro and I made most All-Pro teams at left halfback. I had scored 176 points, far ahead of Don Hutson's old record. I had kicked fifteen out of twenty-eight field goals, and kicked forty-one extra points without a miss. I finished seventh in the league in rushing with 671 yards, and scored the most touchdowns rushing. I completed six of sixteen passes for 118 yards and two touchdowns. I caught twenty-eight passes for 257 yards and two more touchdowns.

So we celebrated and then went back to Green Bay and started studying the Eagles. We sat through movies of their games as Coach and his staff made preparations for the championship game. What it boiled down to is that we figured we could run on them. We were a pretty cocky outfit, we moved the ball against everybody. The thing we were mainly concerned with was their passing, with stopping their quarterback, Norm Van Brocklin.

But we weren't going to change our basic pattern for that game. Usually, the way it went with us on offense, if I ran the ball twelve or thirteen times, that was a lot. Jimmy would run the ball twenty times. Bart would throw thirty passes. That was our offense.

We didn't get in a lot of field practice because it was below zero in Green Bay and the field was frozen solid. We flew to Philadelphia on Saturday and it was cold there. We spent Christmas Eve in our hotel and held a brief workout Christmas Day.

Sunday, December 26, started out cold, but the sun came out about an hour before the kickoff and the temperature at game time was close to forty. We were prepared to wear sneakers but the field was dry and soft enough on top.

I felt very loose kicking off, maybe a little extra adrenalin pouring through there. Tim Brown, who played for us as a

rookie, took the ball to the Eagles' twenty-two. Then, on the
first play, Bill Quinlan knocked the ball out of Van Brocklin's arm and we recovered on the Eagles' fourteen.

We got down to the six and it was fourth and goal and we
didn't get any points out of it. We went for the touchdown
instead of the field goal and Jimmy went in on a slant but
tripped and we were stopped.

We recovered another fumble on the Eagles' twenty-two
and this time I kicked a field goal.

Then we were down deep in their territory again. Bart
called the option play. I moved to my right, saw Boyd Dowler all by himself. He was so wide open I just wanted to stick
it in there instead of just letting it go. I kind of aimed it, and
it was a wobbly throw and they broke it up. So we had to
go for the field goal and we made it and it was 6–0.

In the second quarter Van Brocklin threw twenty-two
yards to Tommy McDonald for a touchdown, then Bobby
Walston kicked a fifteen-yard field goal, and they had us,
10–6.

We moved down to the Eagles' seven but time was running out and we lined up without a huddle to try a field
goal. It was so confusing that there were still two defensive
guys behind us as we lined up. They were hollering and
trying to stall and we needed more time, so we couldn't
center the ball. We didn't know whether we wanted to over-
shift to the right because the ball was from the left hash
mark. It was very confusing. And all of a sudden, the ball
was snapped and I was a little off balance, not quite ready
for it, and I had to hurry the kick. And I missed.

So it was 10–6 at the half but we had moved the ball very
well and we figured we still had a helluva shot at the title. I
thought I was going to have a good day when I came out
for the second half. I ran the ball a few times and got some
good yardage. We went back to the huddle and Bart called

"47," which is the fourth back (me) over the 7 hole (right tackle).

I went through the hole and as I tried to cut back, Chuck Bednarik, the middle linebacker, popped me. His shoulder dug into my side and he was kind of holding me from the left side and the safety man came in and put the finishing tackle on me. And I felt that old familiar twinge in my neck. I fell to the ground, my right arm quivering.

I went out and I figured, hell it's just the pinched nerve and the numbness will go away. I went over to try and throw. I picked up the ball and I couldn't grip the ball. About ten minutes later I tried to throw the ball again, and my arm was just numb. I had no control over it.

I was able to kick, though. Bart hit McGee on a slant for a touchdown and I kicked the extra point and we took the lead, 13–10. Then Ted Dean ran my kickoff back fifty-eight yards to our thirty-nine. And moving mostly on the ground, they went in for the score, and that made it 17–13.

We got down to the Eagles' nine but a field goal would still leave us one point short. Jimmy tried to run the ball in on the game's last play but Bednarik smashed him and that was it.

It was a long plane ride back to Green Bay. You play all year for that one ball game, you know. Coach was feeling bad but he congratulated us and said that we had given it everything we had and that we would be back in the thing next year. And I think we all felt that way.

5. ASK NOT WHAT PAUL HORNUNG CAN DO FOR HIS COUNTRY

It was coming up to Christmastime and I had a game to play on December 31, but it didn't look like I was going to make it. I was stationed in Fort Riley, Kansas, which is like being out on the prairie. There is one good restaurant in the area and nothing else—and that is not to my liking.

Our company was split in half; half were going home the first ten days of the holiday and half the other ten days. I was supposed to leave the first ten days, but that meant I would miss the championship game. So I had to get that changed and I had to get a couple of days' extension. I wanted to get in four or five days of practice before the game, because this was the big one, this was for all the chips.

What to do? I called Coach Lombardi and told him I wasn't going to make it. And Coach got on the phone and called a man named Kennedy in the White House. And the man named Kennedy called another big wheel, and this one called Fort Riley. And in three hours I had my pass.

And that's how I played in that championship game on December 31, 1961, against the New York Giants. And if Coach Lombardi hadn't called President Kennedy, and if John F. Kennedy hadn't made the call he had, I wouldn't have played and wouldn't have won a five-thousand-dollar automobile for being named the most valuable player in the game. I had met President Kennedy several times, once at Notre Dame when he was a senator. I loved that man, and not for what he did for me when I was in a hole. I loved him for what he did for this country in the brief time he had, and I loved him for what he stood for as a man.

But that doesn't explain how I happened to be stuck in Fort Riley in the first place, how I got back into the United States Army. The answer to that is a bit more complicated than you might think, but the immediate catalyst was Berlin.

It was the time of the Berlin crisis. The Russians were threatening war over Berlin, threatening to drive us out of the city. We weren't about to be driven out and President Kennedy had to get tough. And what could be the toughest move for him to make? Why, getting Paul Hornung back in the Army. Late in October of 1961 as the Green Bay Packers rode in first place in the Western Conference having lost but one game, I got my papers ordering me to Milwaukee for a physical.

Up to that point what was simmering in Berlin was furthermost from my mind. My heart and soul was on football exclusively, except for Sunday nights and Monday (and assorted week nights) when I let girls in. So far, it had been a delightful season. We had lost our opener to Detroit, 17–13, but that was all right. Losing opening day games seemed to be a habit with us. Then we really started moving. We beat San Francisco 30–10, we shut out Chicago 24–0. And then, back to back, we put together the finest two professional games I have ever participated in.

In just three years Coach Lombardi had assembled one helluva team. Our offensive blocking, led by center Jim Ringo, and guards Fuzzy Thurston and Jerry Kramer, was out of this world. Forrest Gregg, Bob Skoronski, and Norm Masters were fierce offensive tackles. Ron Kramer in 1961

was at his peak, the best tight end in football. Max McGee
at split end was as cool as always. Boyd Dowler was coming
on strong at flanker.

The defense was just the best in pro football. Willie Davis
and Bill Quinlan were the ends. Hawg Hanner and Hank
Jordan the tackles. Tom Bettis and Ray Nitschke shared middle linebacker, and the corner linebackers—Dan Currie and
Bill Forester—were the best pair any team had. The defensive backfield—Hank Gremminger, Jesse Whittenton, Willie
Wood, and John Symank—was letting nothing through. It
was just a tremendous squad. And I never saw a team with
better discipline, more intelligence, or greater unity of pur-
pose. Every man knew his job and did it in a cool, business-
like manner.

Against Baltimore, on October 8, we were real cool, and
all business.

Three plays after the kickoff, I took a handoff, jabbed my
right foot to the right, putting my weight on that foot and
swinging a shoulder that way to try and fake the linebacker,
then I whipped left. Fuzzy and Jerry and Jimmy were out in
front of me cutting down Colts like stacks of wood, and I
just cut to the outside and headed down the sidelines. Fifty-
four yards and a good run to daylight, as Coach likes to call
it.

Baltimore came right back and scored and then we came
right back and when we got to the thirty-eight they stopped
us temporarily and I kicked the field goal.

A few minutes later we were down there again, this time
on the Baltimore one. I took the handoff for the one-yard
dive over right tackle.

At halftime the score was 17–7, and I had scored all
seventeen points.

Early in the third period Dave Hanner intercepted a
Johnny Unitas pass. Bart Starr went back to pass and I

drifted into the end zone, a secondary receiver. The ends were covered and Bart saw me standing there all alone and he hit me for the touchdown.

Twenty-four points for me so far.

Then we were down on their ten and Bart called for 49 sweep. I started right with Ron, Forrest, and Fuzzy out in front of me. They got me through the line of scrimmage, then I had to cut off tackle and, at about the eight, Artie Donovan and Marv Matuszak were converging on me. Together they weighed five hundred pounds and I couldn't go through them. So I aimed right between them. They had me for one instant, but I broke the tackle and knocked both of them off their feet and kept churning.

There were two more guys waiting for me at the two. When you see another man in a game you figure, here's a chance to hit somebody. You go right into him. That's the game. So I went right into them, and all three of us tumbled into the end zone. That one, I think, was the most satisfying run of my life.

I added two extra points in the fourth period, which made my total thirty-three for the game, a new Packer record. We beat the Colts 45–7 and I can never remember a game when the offensive blocking was so great. The boys really gave me plenty of room to maneuver in.

The following week we were to play Cleveland in Cleveland and that was one we wanted for a lot of reasons. Bill Quinlan, Willie Davis, and Henry Jordan wanted it because they had once played for Cleveland and were never really given a chance to show what they could do. Jimmy Taylor wanted it because he had to prove something to himself —that he could hold his own against the Browns' fullback, Jimmy Brown, the best runner in pro football. Vince Lombardi wanted it because Cleveland was tied for first place in the East and Green Bay was tied for first in the West and it was his skill on the line against the skill of Paul Brown, the most successful coach in pro football history.

Coach told a writer at the time, "We've been preparing for the Browns since last winter, since the day we found out they were on our schedule."

The pressures were a little heavier on some of the boys but the routine that week was the same as always. We relaxed on Sunday night and Monday. We reported at ten in the morning on Tuesday and watched movies of our Baltimore game. The boys were graded as they always are and everyone got high marks for that one.

After the movies there was thirty minutes on the field loosening up, then another thirty minutes listening to scout Wally Cruice tell what Cleveland looked like against the Redskins (they had beaten Washington the previous Sunday, 31–7).

Wednesday morning, Coach gave us our game plan and we split up into groups, offense and defense. The offensive squad went over the thirty or so plays we figured to use against Cleveland, this from a repertoire of two hundred plays. Then we went out on the field and began to shape up and afterwards we went back in and watched movies of Cleveland.

After practice that day I went back home. I was sharing a house in '61 with Jesse Whittenton and Ron Kramer. Max had deserted us (temporarily, as it turned out) by getting married. That night a lot of the guys came over and we cooked roast ducks.

Thursday, the pace began to pick up; the tension, too. We had a long field workout and watched movies. Friday we worked an hour and ten minutes, mostly on goal line plays, and watched more movies.

I was up at seven Saturday morning, drove to the airport, and played gin rummy with Jesse on the flight to Cleveland.

Soon as we got off the plane, we went right out to the stadium for a workout. Coach started on us right there.

"Look at this place," he said, waving his arms at the 78,166 empty seats. "There will be more people here tomorrow than there are in the whole city of Green Bay. Some of you look like you're worried, some of you look like you don't care."

Leave it to Max to have the last word. "Hell, coach," McGee said, "the only thing that scares me is that the Browns may not show up."

They showed up all right, to their everlasting sorrow.

The first time we got the ball we scored. On the Browns' twenty-six, Bart called for the fullback draw. Jimmy took the handoff and headed down the left sideline. I was out in front of him and two defensive backs were coming up. I lowered my shoulder on the first defender and knocked him backward. Jimmy carried the other man the last five yards into the end zone.

The second time we got the ball we scored. The third time we got the ball we scored. It was the biggest offensive performance by a team that I have ever seen in my life.

Bart Starr had the greatest game by a quarterback I ever saw. He hit on fifteen of seventeen passes for 272 yards. One of the two passes he should have completed, I dropped.

Jimmy Taylor had a tremendous game, too. He ended up with 158 yards rushing to seventy-two for Jimmy Brown. He had already scored three touchdowns when we got in close in the fourth period.

Bart came in the huddle, looked at Jimmy, looked at me, and said, "It's Paul's turn, 41 trap." That's a bread-and-butter goal line play, the halfback carrying between the center and right guard, with the guard blocking left.

I said, "Give it to Jimmy this time. It's his day." And Jimmy took it in, his fourth touchdown of the day.

I'm not usually so generous, you know. I've always kidded Jimmy that we would get along fine if he did things my way. I said, "Jim, you can gain all the yards you want. You can run the ball all the way down to the one-yard line, but that's as far as you go 'cause I get paid for bringing it in. So don't you dare take the ball across the end zone."

But Jimmy deserved that one. We beat the Browns 49–17 and our execution was perfect. Afterwards, Coach said it was the best game we ever played and not even Max was going to argue with him.

And after that game I got an unexpected fan letter. I normally receive a hundred or so letters a week during the season, quite a few from females with photos enclosed. But this one came special delivery, registered mail—and no photo. It was from my reserve unit ordering me to Milwaukee for a physical.

I played the following Sunday against Minnesota and, early in the game, aggravated the pinched nerve injury in my neck. Tom Moore filled in and did some job. He carried for 159 yards and we beat the Vikings, 33–7.

Three of us had been called up—Ray Nitschke, Boyd Dowler, and myself. We were all part of the buildup in connection with the Berlin crisis. We were each with different units and I did some checking on my recall. As far as I was able to determine, I was the only fellow out of my control group that was taken. Out of 380 guys, I was the one picked.

I went to Milwaukee for my physical. I had been receiving treatment all week for my neck. The pinched nerve condition actually showed up on X-rays, and the Army had a rule that says if you have anything wrong with your spine and it shows up on an X-ray, you are automatically 4-F. So when I took my physical in Milwaukee, the doctors flunked me.

Naturally I felt happy that I didn't have to go, I wanted to play the season out. I was leading the league in scoring again and the team was leading the league, and we had our minds set on winning the whole thing this year, not just the Western Conference title. We played Minnesota at Milwaukee and won 28–10 and my neck was better. I carried the ball twelve times for seventy yards.

As soon as I got back home I got a call from this general in Minneapolis. "We have received your 4-F papers," he said, "but we want you to go to Great Lakes for a more thorough physical."

Well, actually what they were afraid of was another Mickey Mantle incident. When Mickey first joined the New York Yankees, during the Korean War, he had flunked one physical because of osteomyelitis on his knee. But then his local draft board received letters and they all said the same thing: "How come Mickey Mantle can run like a deer and hit like Babe Ruth and can't serve in the Army?" So Mickey went through hell. He took four or five Army physicals. At the last one, six physicians, including the Fourth Army's orthopedic specialist, examined him carefully. All six doctors agreed that because of osteomyelitis, Mickey was "unacceptable by present Army standards."

The Army apparently didn't want another Mickey Mantle case with me. You know—Hornung's 4-F, but he's still playing football. That would look a little bit too much.

They sent me to Great Lakes and six specialists looked at me for five days. I was a private, and I had six of them, which is quite an honor. Naturally, I knew what they were going to say even before they started. They were going to pass me. If I had flunked there, they would have sent me to Johns Hopkins or somewhere else until I did pass.

My first day at Great Lakes the first specialist looked at me. After about six hours of examination, red tape, signing papers, and all that, I got dressed and shaved to go out. I had my car with me and I had a date waiting for me in Chicago, which is only twenty minutes away. So the Medical Corpsman comes in and says, "Where are you going?"

"I'm going to Chicago."

He says, "No you're not. You can't leave here."

"What do you mean, I can't leave here?"

He said, "Well, you're a patient here and you can't leave."

I said, "Hey, please, look at that paper over there. It says civilian—c-i-v-i-l-i-a-n. I'm not in the Army yet. I'm not part of the Armed Services yet. If I want to go to Chicago and have dinner, I'm going to Chicago."

"Well," he hesitated. "We've got rules. You're not supposed to go."

I told him, "Let's take it up with the captain tomorrow. I don't care if he likes it or not, but I'm not going to stay here for five days and then get drafted in the Army, and I *know* I'm going to get drafted. I'll be back in time for the examination tomorrow morning."

I just did make it back by eight the following morning and the captain, who was a great orthopedic man, was a little angry. He tried to tell me I wasn't supposed to leave the hospital. I said, "Look, there's nothing wrong with me outside of a bad neck and a bad nerve in my neck, but I'm not sick or anything. I'm not in the Army yet. Am I under your authority?"

He admitted I wasn't and I said, "Well, sayonara."

A couple of days later after lots of examinations and X-rays, the captain, the orthopedic specialist, said, "Well, Paul, let me give you some real good advice. You shouldn't think about continuing a football career with that neck. You definitely have a jammed nerve in the cervical spine, which causes a numbness in your right arm, and you have some atrophy in your right arm." Then he continued, "But we're going to give you two or three profiles. If you have a one-four profile, you're a 4-F, see?"

Well, they gave me a two-four profile, then changed it to three, which meant I could go into the service. And so I was in, and they put on my induction papers, "Should begin immediate treatment upon arrival. No prolonged standing, no prolonged lifting, no prolonged sitting"—that type of thing. They didn't want me to do anything strenuous, which means that they were afraid if I got injured with the thing while I was in the Army, that I'd have to get out anyway and then I'd be able to collect disability.

So they ordered me to report to Fort Riley by November 14 and later, when I got out to play some games and anyone mentioned that Hornung was receiving preferential treatment, I could say with perfect logic, "Well, they gave me preferential treatment to get me in there in the first place."

I got in two more games before reporting. I hadn't been able to practice all week because of my physical at Great Lakes and I felt a little rusty against Baltimore. I scored one touchdown on a seventeen-yard run, but Johnny Unitas had a tremendous day, throwing four touchdown passes, and we lost 45–21.

Then we went into Chicago to play the Bears, who were just one game behind us. We rolled in the first half, piling up a 28–7 lead. In the second half, the Bears scored twenty-one points and we scored only three. I kicked a fifty-one-yard field goal, the longest of my career up to the time. That was the margin of the 31–28 victory.

And I was off to save the free world. My housemates, Whittenton and Kramer, recognized the solemnity of the occasion. They put a gold star in the living room window —telling the world that they had yielded a loved one to our country.

I went on to Fort Riley in some style. I had a custom-tailored uniform made for my evenings out at the one restaurant in town. Pat Martin flew me to camp in his private plane, and a friend drove my Cadillac to Kansas, so I would have something to console me. But if I was ever homesick, I was homesick when I got there. What a foul-up it was. All the reservists were going out there and nobody had their uniforms (except me). A lot of the reservist officers had never been in active service before and we just laid around for two weeks in the barracks. We didn't even have any cooks. Guys who had never cooked before were cooking.

I went in as a clerk-typist but they assigned me in this group as a filler to drive a Jeep. Actually, I had to be at the hospital every morning and get treatment on my neck— traction, heat packs, etc.

And then I tried to get a weekend pass back to Green Bay for our next game against the Rams, but I was turned down flat. Most every other N.F.L. player who was recalled got weekend passes to play, but not me. When I found out I wasn't going to get a pass, I raised a little Cain. I told my sergeant, "I want to talk to the general."

Naturally, I had to go through the chain of command. I had to go to my captain and explain my problem to him. And he referred me to the major of the battalion, and the major referred me to the general. I finally got in to see the general and he started talking and after he finished I said, "General, may I be very frank with you?"

Being a democratic general, he said sure.

I said, "General, you've talked to me now for ten minutes and haven't told me one thing. I still can't understand why I'm not getting out. Now I could understand if I was going to miss any duty. But I have this friend of mine who can pick me up in his private plane and fly me out every noon on Saturday and get me back here by midnight on Sunday, and those are the free hours, anyway. And all I would need would be a one-day pass."

The general hemmed and hawed and I kept getting madder and madder. I said, "I can't understand why all the other fellows are getting out and why I'm not. I just want to know. Am I to assume it's coming from higher up?"

And he said, "Yes, Fifth Army headquarters."

I said, "What can we do about it?"

He said, "I don't know. I'll have to check with General ———."

Turns out there was an actual directive that said no pass for Hornung. I missed that Los Angeles game, which we won, and later I missed the Los Angeles game on the Coast. But otherwise, my hell-raising did some good and I got my pass to play on weekends.

My first game as Private Paul Hornung was Thanksgiving Day against the Lions. Naturally, I was a little rusty. My timing was off and I was hitting holes either too soon or too late. They had us 9–7 at the half and I hadn't done a thing. In the third quarter we got down to the Detroit thirty and Bart went back to pass and I slipped down the sidelines and caught it in the right corner and went down to the four. Jimmy bucked in and we went ahead of the Lions. I kicked a nine-yard field goal with twenty-eight seconds left and that gave us a 17–9 victory. And the next day I was as sore as I had ever been in my life.

Naturally, I wasn't able to practice much but I did keep in shape at camp. My habits in the Army were terrible. I ate regular meals, I got up at a certain time in the morning. I got to bed mostly at the same time at night. The life wasn't exactly to my liking but at least it helped keep me in shape and I was ready to play each Sunday.

With three games left we had a 9–2 record and all we needed was one victory in our last three games to wrap it

up. And the toughest one was coming up against the New
York Giants, who were fighting for the Eastern title.

We won it 20–17 to sew up the Conference title. Jimmy
Taylor had a tremendous day with 186 yards in twenty-
seven carries, a new rushing record for the Packers. I gained
fifty-four yards in eleven rushes. My timing was still off but
I blocked better in that game, I think, than I ever had. We
moved the ball so well against the Giants that I think most of
us hoped they'd be our opponent in the championship game.

I made the San Francisco trip and we got beat 22–21, and
that was my last regular-season game. They wouldn't let me
off for the Rams' game which we won, 24–17, to conclude
another happy season.

It was happy for everybody, but especially so for the nine
Packers who made the various All-Pro teams: Jim Ringo,
Dan Currie, Fuzzy Thurston, Jimmy Taylor, Forrest Gregg,
Hank Jordan, Jesse Whittenton, Bill Forester, and myself.
The biggest honor for me came when the Associated Press,
in a poll of sportswriters and newscasters, named me as the
N.F.L.'s most valuable player. I was at the Fort when I got
the news and I was really surprised. I had missed two games
and I felt my play had suffered being in the Army. But I
had ended up leading the league in scoring for the third
straight year with 146 points. I rushed 127 times for 597
yards and a 4.7 average. I completed three of five passes
for forty-two yards, caught fifteen passes for 145 yards,
kicked fifteen field goals in twenty-two attempts, and ex-
tended my extra-point record to eighty-two in a row.

And the New York Giants did win the Eastern Conference
title and we had two weeks to get ready for the big one.
That is, the *team* had two weeks to get ready. I almost didn't
make it to the game at all and I wouldn't have if President
Kennedy hadn't asked not what Paul Hornung could do for
his country, but what his country could do for Paul Hornung.

Pat Martin came flying to pick me up ten days before the big one. With him was Phil Rochon, president of Green Bay Aviation. Phil always came along when there was a danger of bad weather, and the weather wasn't too good when we took off in a borrowed Cessna 310 (Pat's was being fixed). And as soon as we got up, the weather turned real poor.

The plane didn't have on icing boots and we couldn't get over the weather. Ice was forming on the wings and we went up to twelve thousand feet to beat it and couldn't get over it and we went from twelve thousand to three thousand feet in about a minute and a half. I was scared to death. We flew around in that funk from walnut tree to walnut tree and we didn't know where in the hell we were. We couldn't get anybody on the radio because of static and we were flying blind.

I started praying, my hands started sweating, and my whole life started parading in front of me. Phil just kept jerking the props, trying to knock the ice off the wings, and it was getting real bad. And I said to Pat and Phil, *"Get this crate on the ground."* All I wanted to do was hook it on the back of a Hertz Rent a Car.

Somehow, Pat and Phil did get us down. We landed safely in Rochester, Minnesota, in twenty inches of snow, skidding all the way off the runway. Soon as I got on the ground I made a few salaams and, thinking of the fiancée who was coming in to see me from Milwaukee, I said to Pat, "I'm calling my girl and tell her to stay in Milwaukee. I've changed my way of living. From now on, nothing bad. No way."

We rented a car and got into Green Bay about nine that evening, and the first stop we made was at Speed's bar. We needed something for our nerves. All of the boys were there and they didn't expect me. Bill Quinlan saw me first and grabbed the microphone and hoisted himself atop the bar.

He hollered into that mike at the top of his voice: "A.W.O.L. Paul is back!" Then he stepped back and almost fell off the bar.

Here I was, trying to keep quiet and everything, and Quinny was yelling and screaming and hollering, and he grabbed me and lifted me off the floor and we had a great swinging night.

The next day, red-eyed, I went out to try and get ready for the big game.

6. "TODAY YOU WERE THE GREATEST TEAM"

I got with Red Cochran, our backfield coach, right away and he gave me a list of plays for the championship game and explained the changes that had been made in our offense. By this time of the year, nothing changes very much. We were going to do the regular things against the Giants that we always tried to do against all the teams— block and tackle people, try to run on 'em, try to pass some.

And we were very, very confident. Even though we had only beaten the Giants 20–17 a month earlier, we had controlled the ball the entire game. I think we had about 270 yards rushing, 180 yards passing. Our offensive line had handled the Giant defense pretty easy. So we were feeling good about our chances. All we wanted to do was play our own ball game and let the Giants play their ball game.

Not everyone was in perfect shape for the Giants and that was one small worry. In the Los Angeles game, Jimmy Taylor suffered a painful rib injury and was still hurting. Max had sore ribs, too. They would play with those little hurts, naturally, but they might not be 110 per cent effective, the way Coach likes. But the rest of the team was in good shape and I personally felt real good. I had had enough time and practice to regain the timing I had lost, and I felt my co-

ordination was as sharp as if I had been just plain Paul
Hornung, civilian, rather than Paul Hornung, Pfc.

Ron Kramer's wife, Nancy, and the children came in for
the game, so Jesse and I—knights at heart—gave the Kramers
the house and we moved into the Downtowner Motel. My
mother got in two days before the game and stayed at the
Downtowner, too. The Giants arrived on Saturday, December 30, and they were at the Northland Hotel. That night,
Jesse, Dapper Dan Currie, and myself had dinner with some
of the Giants at the Spot. Del Shofner, the Giants' offensive
end, had roomed with Jesse when they played with the
Rams and they were kidding each other pretty good.

"Jesse," Del said, "I'm going to do everything you do and
go everywhere you go tonight and have fun and then tomorrow I'm going to run your legs off."

Well, we didn't do much. We were back at the Downtowner well before the 11 P.M. curfew and, like I always do,
I managed a restful, dreamless night of sleep.

I awoke Sunday morning, the last day of 1961, and looked
out the window. The sun was shining and that made me
feel better. It had snowed early in the week and the temperature all week had never risen above sixteen and we
had had to wear tennis shoes at all our practice sessions.
We preferred a good, dry field.

I had breakfast with Mom and we went to Mass together
and then I left her at the motel and drove to the stadium.

It was eleven o'clock when I started dressing for the
game. I like to take my time dressing and this day was no
exception. I pulled on my gold pants with the green and
white piping on the legs. I slipped my No. 5 jersey over my
neck, which measures seventeen and a half inches and
means custom-made shirts. I started to put on my cleats but
changed my mind and put on tennis shoes. "Anybody seen
the field yet?" I yelled.

One of the guys said, "They're taking the hay off now. Looks like it's in pretty good shape."

"What's the temperature?"

"Close to twenty."

"I'm sweating just thinking about it."

Ron Kramer, whose locker is next to mine, came in and grinned at me. "Just stay behind me, baby," he said, "and you'll win yourself a new Corvette."

Max McGee, with that habitual bored look on his face, sat at his locker philosophizing. "Everybody look pretty," he said. "There's gonna be twenty million people watching us on TV."

"How many of them are female?" someone, not me, inquired.

"Maybe five million."

"And the Horn knows half of them," Max said.

"Better believe it," I grinned. There was no undue tension in that room at all. The boys seemed very loose. The joking went on, most of it unprintable and most of the language censorable. They were just getting up for the thing, and the air was sweet with confidence.

Outside, the town of Green Bay was slightly hysterical. On an average football Sunday, the sixty-seven thousand residents are normally off-balance. But this was the first title game in the history of the town and New Year's Eve was beginning early. It would end early, too, if we lost.

We went out and loosened up as we always did—some calisthenics, then a passing drill. I practiced place-kicking, starting at the twenty and moving back gradually and switching from one side of the field to the other, until I was kicking the ball from the forty-five-yard line. The wind was blowing about ten miles an hour, no real factor.

At twelve forty-five, fifteen minutes before kickoff time, we were back in the dressing room and Coach was giving us his usual pep talk. He was neither more nor less eloquent than he always is before a game. But we felt it more because the stakes were higher—some five thousand dollars for the winning team, to three thousand dollars for the losers.

"I know you can win," he said. "You should have won the championship last year and you know it. So let's not make any mistakes. This game means a lot to all of you—in money and in prestige. Be alert—let's get them!"

Coach and his assistants retired and we were left alone with the offensive captain, Jim Ringo, and defensive captain, Bill Forester, leading a quick meeting. Each of us were invited to speak. Each of us did. I had nothing vital to say, no great message for the world. "Let's go, gang," I hollered. "Let's get 'em quick." That was the idea, put it to them right away.

We ran out on the field and the roar from the crowd was like John Philip Sousa music washing over us. Forty thousand people out there and all of them, I think, expected nothing less than victory from us.

The field seemed firm as I spotted the ball on the tee, preparing to kick off. The kick went down to the goal line and the return was insignificant. On the first play from scrimmage, Y. A. Tittle handed off to Joel Wells and Wells tried to go outside our left tackle, and Henry Jordan came across and smashed him down for a one-yard gain. And three plays later they were kicking to us, and as soon as I came onto the field, I could just sense something. It's a little hard to explain, but I just felt we were going to have one hell of a day.

I carried three times on that first series, with Jimmy acting as decoy, and made a total of nine yards. So we had to kick to the Giants. And that was the only time we kicked that first half.

The Giants moved close to midfield, then Kyle Rote dropped a pass deep in our territory and they had to kick.

We took the ball on our twenty. The Giants were in a five-man line at this point, which was a new wrinkle; they had always played the traditional 4–3 defense. So Bart, compensating, sent me through the strong side of our line, with Ron Kramer blocking in on the tackle and Forrest Gregg, Ringo, and Bob Skoronski out in front. The first time we had played the Giants, we had chewed up the right side of their line. Now we were working on the left side.

I went four yards on the first carry, then Bart dropped back to pass and I slipped downfield and Bart hit me at midfield for a twenty-six-yard pickup.

I ran for five more yards, then Jimmy hit three times for thirteen yards, and then I went off tackle for seven more and a first down on the twenty-five. The quarter ended three plays later and we were sitting on the Giants' six-yard line.

On the first play of the quarter, I took the handoff from Bart and hit off right tackle. I think the thing that always helped my ball-carrying more than anything was intelligence, knowing how to cut and when to cut. I'm not a real fast back and I don't have the Jim Brown or Jim Taylor type of power, so a lot depends on intelligence. If I hit off right tackle and the hole turns out to be over right guard I have to be quick enough to see it, and know the right moment to cut, and I've always been called a good cutback runner.

On this play I didn't have to use too much intelligence. The blocking was there. Jim Ringo brushed the Giants' middle linebacker, Sam Huff, with a soft block and then Ron came over and surprised Sam by hitting him hard and preventing him from swinging wide on this play to the strong side. And I went in for the score. I kicked the point and it was 7–0.

Our defense was putting a lot of pressure on Tittle and on the next series, Henry Jordan deflected a pass and Ray Nitschke picked it off and we were back in scoring territory.

We got down to their thirteen and Bart dropped back and led Boyd Dowler perfectly and Boyd stretched and caught the ball at full speed and went in for the score. And it was 14–0 after I kicked the point.

Another interception, this time by Hank Gremminger, set up our third touchdown. The ball was on the fourteen and Bart called for a flood right. This is designed to pull the middle linebacker to his left to help in handling a flood of receivers to that side. Ron, playing tight end, blocks hard enough on the corner linebacker so that he gets the idea that Kramer is not going to be a pass receiver. The linebacker's natural reaction is to fight off the block and release Kramer. If he felt Ron was to be the pass receiver, naturally he would try to hold him. So Tom Scott released Kramer, Huff ran to his right leaving the middle clear, and Kramer was there and Bart hit him and he took three Giants with him in the end zone.

With one play left in the half I kicked a seventeen-yard field goal and we went off the field with a 24–0 margin.

The second half was just as easy. I kicked a twenty-two-yard field goal. Ron caught another touchdown pass, this one on a picture-book thirteen-yard throw from Starr. And I kicked a nineteen-yard field goal. And we had won the game and the N.F.L. championship, 37–0.

In the dressing room before he let anyone in, Coach Lombardi made a little speech. You could see he was moved. He kept wiping at his glasses. He said, "Today, you were the greatest team in the history of the National Football League." And that sentence really hit us, really sank in.

Then the doors opened and we were flooded with reporters and television people and well-wishers. Someone from *Sport* Magazine came over and said I had won the Chevrolet Corvette given each year to the most valuable player in the game. I was surprised. Ron, in the next stall, was sipping on a pint of whiskey brought in by his dad. He shook hands with me and he didn't even seem to mind when the representative from *Sport* said that if Hornung hadn't won it, Ron would have. "And I had to tell you to follow me," he said.

Truthfully, Ron deserved the car as much as I. A lot of guys deserved it. Our defense held the Giants to only thirty yards on the ground. Willie Davis, Quinlan, Hawg Hanner, and Henry Jordan put tremendous pressure on the Giant quarterback. Our secondary intercepted four passes. Our offensive line just blew the defense out of there. Bart called a magnificent game. But I suppose I had the statistics on my side. My nineteen points was a new playoff game scoring record. I rushed for eighty-nine yards on twenty carries. I caught three passes for forty-seven yards and kicked three field goals. But this was a team victory in every way, not an individual victory.

That night we welcomed in the New Year with happiness in our hearts, but I have had wilder New Year's Eves. Pat and Mary Ellen Martin held a dinner party at their home and a lot of the guys were there—Dan Currie, Ron and Nancy Kramer, Jesse and his girl, Boyd Dowler and his date. Mom was with her two closest gal friends from Louisville, Lil and Jinx, and I had a little fiancée with me. And we stayed there and ate and drank and toasted in the New Year and then we went into town to see the celebrating.

It was something. The town of Green Bay had gone absolutely berserk. One, two in the morning, automobiles were tooting through the city with hands pressed on horns. Old men and old women, young men and young women, kids, were reveling in the streets. We dropped in at a dance honoring the Lombardis and I've never seen Coach look happier, or Mrs. Lombardi more radiant. It was their night.

From the dance we made the rounds of our favorite watering spots. Eveywhere we went, they were standing six deep at the bar. One place we did manage to get up close and have a drink with the crowd, and then Ron had to take command to get us out. He put out that big, hamlike hand of his, stretched to his full six feet four, 260 pounds, and hollered, "We're coming through. If anyone gets in our way, I'll kill 'em; it's as simple as that."

Well, it wasn't that simple but we fought our way through and I had to fight off the women who wanted to plant a victory kiss on my kisser, and sometimes they succeeded (most of the time, in fact). I didn't fight them too hard and my date was understanding. It was an occasion, you know.

And then the noise and the madness got to be too much and it was just too crowded and I took my date home and I went home and slept through most of New Year's Day. And if I had dreams that night, they had to be pleasant ones.

Looking back now, looking back to that December 31, 1961, I am struck by the significance of that date in my life. It was our first championship. It was a personal high point in my career. We would win again in 1962 but for various reasons it would not be like 1961. And I would be sitting out the 1963 season, and 1964 would be a disappointment. So now that last day of the year 1961, that day when we were freshly crowned champions and could do no wrong, has taken on fresh dimensions.

A couple of days into the new year of 1962, the party was over. Pfc. Paul Hornung was back at Fort Riley.

The 1962 season was a troubled one for me on several counts. For one thing I was stuck in the Army right up until the time I was to report for practice, in July of 1962. For another, I began to feel the first forebodings over my betting on football games. And I spent a good part of the season on the sidelines because of a knee injury.

I've got no complaints over my Army duty at Fort Riley. I was assigned to the public information office and everyone treated me very well. I had an office over in the Army museum, and I had every weekend off, from Friday to Sunday. I went to Kansas City a couple of times, I went to the Coast a few times, I picked up a plaque in Wisconsin as that state's athlete of the year, and a plaque in Kentucky as *that* state's athlete of the year. I went to Miami to model clothes for Jantzen and I even made it to the Kentucky Derby. My social life hardly suffered, but still I was in the Army and I couldn't do everything I wanted to do. I wasn't free and I love my freedom.

It was good, soft duty and that was the trouble. I reported in terrible condition that July.

It wasn't that I was too heavy, but I just didn't have my legs in shape; they were like lead pipes. Coach took one close look at me that first day and I could see he wasn't too happy with what he saw.

"What do you weigh?" he said.

"Oh, about 222. I'm only seven pounds over."

"Good."

The fifth day of practice was very hot and we were wearing T-shirts and shorts and Coach lined our kicking team against our receiving team. I was the deep man in the end zone. The ball came to me and I took it five yards deep and started upfield. The first fifteen yards were negotiable but when I hit the twenty, I was feeling terrible. I was trying to get my knees up and the effort was just too much.

Coach started hollering at me. "All the way! All the way!" And the players on the sidelines were whistling and putting me on and it was like I was back at Notre Dame and they were inflicting the whistle drill on me again, and I practically crawled to the goal line.

Coach came over to me and said, "Well, I guess you got the news."

"I got it," I muttered. I could hardly talk and the sweat was pouring off my face.

"That was ludicrous," Coach said. "That was absurd. What have you been doing with yourself?"

"I don't know. I don't know." And I didn't. All I knew was I was woefully out of shape. I played in the exhibition games and I still wasn't right and Coach wasn't too happy. I remember one game in late August against the Cardinals, I picked up a total of eleven yards in eight carries.

It was about this time, too, that Pete Rozelle, the N.F.L. Commissioner, had his first private talk with me, warning me about my associations. And that's when I smelled that something was wrong, and that's when I stopped betting on football games.

So I came up to our opening football game against the Minnesota Vikings just a bit low in spirits. I am an optimist but before that game I wasn't at my most optimistic.

Things got better right away, though.

My first touchdown was six yards through a hole at right guard, with Fuzzy knocking out the end. My second touchdown was seven yards through a hole at right tackle, with Fuzzy obliterating the end again. I kicked a ten-yard field goal, and a forty-five-yard field goal. I threw a forty-one-yard pass to Boyd Dowler. Late in the third period I had twenty-one points and we were down in their territory once again, on the thirty-seven.

Bart called for a dive-right, with Jim Taylor slanting off tackle. But when he came up on the line, Bart noticed the linebackers were shifted left and the right corner linebacker was inside the right tackle. He called the audible. Now I was to get the ball.

Starr faked the handoff to Jim, who hit dutifully at right

tackle. Bart slipped me the ball and I was in motion to my left, looking for daylight. I got it when Jerry Kramer, who was pulling in front of me, hit Jim Marshall, the defensive end—just creamed him—and Marshall was gone, and I cut right and shot past the line of scrimmage. Forrest Gregg, moving downfield from right tackle position, flattened the Minnesota safetyman and I was in all alone.

We beat Minnesota 34–7 and my twenty-eight points was the second best scoring performance of my pro career, and one of the most satisfying. In the dressing room Henry Jordan came over, patted me, and said, "Sonofagun, we thought we were saving you for the prom, but you were just waiting for the gong."

Jerry Kramer gave me a great big bear hug and I gave it right back. "I sprung you loose," he hollered. "I got a block. I trapped an end." He sure did. If Kramer doesn't block, Hornung doesn't score. I scored three touchdowns and in all three the guards were responsible.

And it looked like another beautiful season ahead, and it was for a while. The next three games only one touchdown was scored against us. We beat St. Louis 17–0. We beat the Bears 49–0. We beat Detroit 9–7. And Minnesota coming up again.

It happened early. It was an off-tackle play and Fuzzy, in front of me, didn't get out of the hole and pull fast enough and Cliff Livingston red-dogged from linebacker and he just flew through the air and hit my knee just as I was planting my right foot. And he just bent it all the way when my weight was going forward. So I was out of there and they took X-rays and they found I had a wrenched knee and torn ligaments in the knee.

I didn't kick for the rest of the season and I didn't play much, either. I did get in the last two games and that was it. All told I carried just fifty-seven times, for 219 yards.

But the team played magnificently. We were winning every week, mostly by big scores. We beat the Eagles 49–0 in one game and gained 628 yards on total offense. As we walked off the field at halftime, Eagle linebacker Chuck Bednarik asked our end coach, Tom Fears, "Tom, when are you going to put in the scrubs?"

Tom looked right through Bednarik. "Chuck," he said, "we don't have any scrubs."

Detroit was the only team able to beat us, but we dominated everything. We led the league in total offense, were second in total defense, and almost everyone was named All-Pro—Ron Kramer, Forrest Gregg, Jerry Kramer, Fuzzy, Jim Ringo, Jim Taylor, Willie Davis, Henry Jordan, Dan Currie, Bill Forester, Herb Adderley. Jimmy Taylor just had a tremendous year. He led the league in scoring, and he beat out Jim Brown for the rushing title.

And there was a return match with the New York Giants for the N.F.L. title.

It was Green Bay weather in New York. The temperature at game time was seventeen degrees and must have dropped to ten before the end. The wind was blowing in gusts of thirty-five miles an hour. The field was like concrete.

And, again, we were the better team.

We opened the scoring late in the first quarter when Bart directed the team down to the nineteen and Jerry Kramer kicked a twenty-six-yard field goal. In the second period, Ray Nitschke recovered a fumble on the Giant twenty-eight. Then I got in one of my few moments of the season. On the option pass I hit Dowler on the seven for a twenty-one-yard gainer. Bart then called Jim's number and he took the ball and no one was going to stop him. He just stormed through and over bodies, high-kneeing it into the end zone.

In the third period the Giants moved up close. They

blocked a kick and Jim Collier fell on it in the end zone and now we were ahead only 10–7.

But Ray Nitschke (who was to win the Corvette, rightfully, as the game's most valuable player) saved us again with another fumble recovery and Jerry kicked a twenty-nine-yard field goal, and it was 13–7.

We moved the ball gradually downfield in the fourth quarter. My eighth carry of the day was my best. I set up Jerry's last field goal by taking the 49 sweep around right end for eleven yards. But I got smacked hard and hurt my knee again and that was it for me.

That was it for me, in fact, for nineteen months, until July of 1964. Nineteen long months, counting that twelve-month sabbatical. And the first time I got to run the ball in a game after my suspension, that first play was in our annual intra-squad game at Green Bay, and there were twenty thousand people watching.

And it was the same play that had ended the 1962 season for me, 49 sweep around right end. And this time I made twenty-two yards. And it was good to be back.

Part IV

1. MAX

My closest friend in football today is Max McGee, and he has been since 1957, the year I broke in with the Packers. That summer, Max met us at Greensboro, North Carolina, after his discharge from the Air Force. Captain McGee came right up to me, a tall, handsome guy with a world-weary look on his face.

"Let me look at you, Heisman," he said. He was an end, you know, and he was sizing me up. "The quarterback's got to make me a living," he explained.

Right after that we had a scrimmage and I was quarterback and I remember on one play, I reared back with that Notre Dame arm that wasn't yet housebroken and whipped the ball out in the flat, intended for Max. Only it went into the stands. Back in the huddle, Max gave me a disdainful stare.

"Listen, man," he said, "you gonna throw me the ball or throw souvenirs all day long."

We hit it off right away. Max and I roomed together on the road and at home we rented a house together with Billy Howton. And naturally since Max was single (though he had been married) and I was single we went out on the town together. And the only year we weren't together was 1961, the year Max lived with his second wife.

We have shared fines together for skipping out after curfew, and we have more than once avoided fines simply by
not getting caught. And we have carved out many a ball in
different towns all over the U.S.A. We've always liked the
same things. He likes girls, and nice clothes, and nice times
and entertainment. He's free with a dollar. I mean, he'll go
for anything. He's a real swinging guy.

One night in Los Angeles we were entertaining a couple
of ladies in our room when one of the coaches knocked for
bed check. It was a very chilly night but we hustled the
ladies out on the veranda, and they were standing out there
freezing while the coach came in and jawed with us awhile,
looking around the room suspiciously. He probably was wondering how come all of a sudden we were using perfume.
But we were able to get him out of there and as soon as he
left, we called the girls. They came in, teeth chattering, they
were so cold. And we smuggled them out of the hotel.

The business of training camp has especially bugged Max.
We have roomed together at St. Norbert's College (about
ten miles from Green Bay), Room 120, Sensenbrenner Hall.
It is hot in the month of August and we sometimes get restless. You know, after you're in training camp awhile, it gets
you kind of edgy. You're with these guys every day, twelve
hours a day, so you have to have a little fun together.

So one Saturday night we were in town and we were dis-
turbed to have to interrupt our pleasure to make eleven
o'clock curfew. You get three hours out a week that one
night and you want to have a good time.

Well, one of the coaches always comes around and makes
bed check, and we knew Red Cochran, the backfield coach,
was checking this particular night.

We made it back just before curfew, took off our clothes,
pulled our beds together, and turned off the lights. And it
was about eleven and it was very quiet and there we were,

with our arms around each other and holding each other. And Red opened the door, flipped on the lights, and it kind of hit him right in the face.

We both just looked at him straight-faced and said, "Would you just please turn off the lights and shut the door, we're busy now." And Red almost flipped. He shut the door for just a minute, he was so flabbergasted. We got up and called him back and we were roaring. He knew we had been kidding but the shock really hit him. But that didn't stop him or the other coaches from taking bed check every damned night.

Max actually is a very droll, very funny guy. He's the one who told a writer, "Hornung's got a forty-three-inch chest and a thirty-six-inch head." He said it as a joke (I think) but every writer who has ever done a story about me has used it, just as I'm using it here. Max always explained, "I'm doing everything I can to project the Golden Boy's public image."

One night we were at a club in L.A. and we had just taken over the bandstand and were up singing. And Max looked over at me and said, "With my voice and your moves we could go places." He meant my moves on the bandstand; I was doing a little twisting. Then he looked at me again and with a small grin on his face he said, "With my personality and your good looks."

He is a very good needler. One summer when we were reunited at training camp I took a look at McGee and said, "You're going to be put on the fat man's training table."

Max said, "Then you and I will be eating together."

Later that same afternoon after a workout, I stripped off a torn jersey. "See," I said to McGee, "it's torn on the back. That shows that they're pulling at me after I'm past them. They don't get me from the front."

McGee said solemnly, "Why don't you start going into the line head first instead of rear first?"

One day one of the Packer players borrowed Max's new car and he thought it had been stolen and reported it to the police. They called him back a few hours later and said that it was parked in the front window of a downtown department store.

"So how much furniture have we bought?" Max said.

The year of my sabbatical, when I went up to Green Bay before the start of the season, I called a meeting of all the players. "Fellas," I said, "during my year's sabbatical, Max is taking over for me. He is to have all my girls on the circuit." Not that he can't do it on his own. He swings pretty good. When we were in Miami for the Playoff Bowl in January of 1965, someone asked Max:

"What are you going to do after the game?"

Max said, "There's still twenty-four girls I haven't seen down here. It'll take me three days to get through them."

He's very witty and just a great guy to be with. I mean, he's got great manners. He fits in a real swinging, loose, uninhibited crowd, and he would fit in right at the Inaugural party for the President of the United States. He is very very fast on his feet. His idea of making out with the girls is, "I might not be good-looking but all I need is about twenty minutes to show you how charming and fantastic I am." That's actually his philosophy and he comes pretty close to being right, he makes out so well.

Max comes from Texas naturally, from a large family. He had an older brother, Coy McGee, who was a halfback at Notre Dame before me. Coy was a brilliant student and graduated *magna cum laude* in Chemical Engineering and now he has an important position in the aircraft industry. Max is intelligent, too, but he was never inclined to push himself too hard. He went to Tulane on an athletic scholarship and even as a freshman he was working nights tending bar at one of New Orleans' Latin Quarter establishments.

When the Packers drafted Max in 1954 he was a 6-2, 200-pound halfback but they converted him to an end. And he became a good one. I don't think anybody's got any better moves than Max, and he cuts real well. Coach himself always felt that Max could have been a super receiver if he were a perfectionist. In his book *Run to Daylight!* Vince Lombardi wrote about Max, "He can relax before, during and after a game, and it makes him a great player, although it also contributes to his tendency to be a little careless. . . . I've seen him drop the easy pass and make the great one-hander. All receivers will do that, of course, but Max more than most."

I remember one time on the option I was moving to my right and saw Max downfield, free. I let the ball go and it was away from him and he made a great one-handed tumbling catch in the end zone. And afterwards a sportswriter asked him about it.

"Hornung is supposed to make me look good on those," Max said. "On that one, he made me look ridiculous."

Well, I always told Max, "When I throw you a pass, I want you to step out on the one-yard-line so I can score." Funny thing is, he did get knocked out on the one a few times. And he'd come back and say, "There it is, Paulie, go get it."

Max loves to have the ball thrown to him and he always gets dejected when the quarterback won't throw him the ball. He's the kind of guy if he were open and they weren't throwing to him, he wouldn't come back and say, "I can beat this square out or cut in," or anything like that. He'll just brood. "The hell with it," he'll say. "If you don't want to throw it to me, don't."

Another thing about Max, he's superstitious.

When he was punting for the Packers, he used to worry

something crazy. "I'm going to drop it," he said, "I'm going to drop it."

One day I really got on him. I told him, "You know, I had a dream last night."

"What dream?"

"I dreamed it was the fourth quarter and it was a real tight ball game and Bart hit you with a beautiful pass right in the end zone and you dropped the ball, and we blew the game —boom!"

"Oh, you're crazy," Max said. Well, sure enough, we were playing in Milwaukee and it was a very tight ball game going to the third or fourth quarter. Bart hit him with a pass and all he had to do was catch it and step into the end zone, and he drops the ball. Max comes back and says, "You and your damned dream." He actually blamed me for dropping the ball.

So after that, any time I wanted to do anything, I had a way to get Max to do it. Once we were getting ready to go out to dinner and I said, "I want to eat at the Spot."

Max said, "No, I want to eat in the Stratosphere." That's another fancy restaurant just outside of Green Bay.

"I had a dream," I said.

"Okay," Max said, "let's eat in the Spot."

When we were in New York in 1962 for the championship game, I said to Max, "Why don't you go to Mass with me?"

Max is a Baptist and he said, "No, it's cold. I want to just lay around and keep my legs loose."

I said, "Well, you've never seen St. Patrick's Cathedral here. You ought to go. Because this is a real big visiting spot, a landmark in New York, a lot of people visit the place."

And he said, "No, no, no."

And I said, "Well, I had a dream last night."

And he said, "What time is Mass?"

So I got him over to Mass and at Mass like any religious ceremony, there was a collection. Max was just sitting there and watching us get up and down, up and down, and all of a sudden about six ushers got up and start taking up a collection. And I reached in my pocket and got out a dollar bill, and Max reached in his wallet and got out a bill and threw it in the basket.

About ten minutes later—why, here they go again, coming up for a second collection. And Max was looking a little more quizzical now. I reached in my pocket and he reached in there and he grabbed a bill out of my wallet for the collection.

Just about five minutes before the Mass was over, here they go again, another collection (two's enough in Kentucky). I can't look at Max now. I don't know what he's going to think now. The usher got about three or four pews from us and I got a real cute little elbow in the ribs.

"What the hell are they going to do now," Max says, "search us?"

In the early spring of '65 Max opened up a restaurant in Manitowoc, across the peninsula from Green Bay. It's called "The Left End" and I went up there for the opening night formalities. Business was terrific and we had a ball and Max, who had been working for a guy in Texas, seemed very pleased. "I'm going to Texas for a few days," he told the fellas who were running the place for him, "and I'll be back in a couple of days."

Four weeks later he still hadn't returned, and no one knew where he was or how to get hold of him. But that's Max. It's not that he's irresponsible. There are a lot of things he just doesn't give a damn about. He had something like a $250,-000 life insurance policy through the Air Force and he let the thing lapse simply because he just wouldn't answer his mail to find out that his premium was due. And sometimes he gets in a jam doing things like that.

But you're not going to change Max. I think Marie Lombardi's description of Max is maybe the most apt. She says there's an air of mystery about Max. There is, too, but I'll tell you this. One of the things I'm going to miss about football when I'm no longer in it, or when Max or myself get traded off the Packers, I'm going to miss that close relationship I had with Max. He's an original.

2. THE BEST MEN

In going over the football players I consider to be the best in my time, you will have to forgive me for including so many Green Bay Packers. I believe that in the last five or six years, we have had more great football players than any other team in professional football. Besides, they all contributed to making Paul Hornung, like Wyatt Earp, a legend in his own time.

Several years ago a magazine ran a story on Fuzzy Thurston, our offensive guard. The title was: "The Man Who Made Paul Hornung." It's true. If Fuzzy doesn't block, Hornung doesn't score. Fuzzy made me; Jerry Kramer, our other offensive guard, made me; Jim Ringo, our center, made me; Jim Taylor made me; Bart Starr made me. And the defensive team, who got us the ball to run for sixty-five plays a game made me. Someone, it seems, was always making me.

My one other qualification about the men I am going to name is that the majority of them come from the Western Conference. We play only two regular games a season with Eastern Conference players, so I'm much more aware of Western Conference players. But it's also true that in recent years the All-Pro teams have been made up mostly of Western Conference players.

Anyway, these are my best—offensive team first.

FULLBACK

Jimmy Brown, naturally. Jimmy is probably the best athlete in the country today. He could have been great at any
sport he chose. He could play pro baseball, pro basketball.
He could probably have been heavyweight boxing champion
of the world if he wanted to box. Just a real natural. It has
to be something in his physical makeup because Jimmy
never gets hurt. As many times as you carry the football,
you've got to get hurt. I mean, you have guys 285 pounds
who get hurt. But Jimmy Brown never gets hurt. He's got
230 pounds on him and not an ounce of fat on him and he's
built like a llama and runs like a llama—swoosh, he takes
off and he's gone.

There have been knocks against Jimmy that he doesn't
block. I remember when a reporter put this question to him,
Jimmy said, "I'm not paid to block." I think it's a little far-
fetched. If Jimmy Brown has to block, he's going to block. I
don't think he's out there trying not to block. I think if he
lined up across from you with a definite blocking assignment,
that he'd do a helluva job of blocking you.

The big difference between Jim Brown and Jimmy Taylor,
my No. 2 fullback, is that Brown has a lot more speed. He
combines great power with great speed and that's an un-
beatable combination. Jimmy Taylor is quicker at hitting a
hole and he's a little bit better finding a hole than Brown, but
he doesn't have Brown's speed. In other words, Brown will
break clear for more big plays than Taylor will. He'll run the
ball a little more than Taylor, too. When the year's statistics
are in, Taylor has his twelve hundred yards and maybe
Brown has fourteen hundred and that's the way it's always
been, except for 1962. That year Jimmy Taylor was the finest
fullback in the country. It's like in basketball, if you want to
form the ideal team, where do you start? You start with Bill

Russell. It's the same way in football. If you want to form the ideal team, you start with Jimmy Brown.

Howie Ferguson, who was in his twilight when I first came up to the Packers, was another fullback I respected very much. He was a tough, tough sonofagun. I used to watch him get his knee maimed maybe three times a week. He'd go out on Sunday and run over people. He didn't have any great speed and he didn't cut that well, but he was such a bull and he had so much in his heart.

Another fullback who was the same way was Alex Webster of the New York Giants. Webster was the kind of guy who would give you 120 per cent at all times. He was a real money ballplayer. If they needed three yards, they had to go to Webster. He was the kind of ballplayer pro coaches admire because he played with small injuries. A small injury is this: No matter how badly you are injured, the coach defines it as small. I mean, he thinks it's small. "Well, you take it easy all week," he says, "but you'll be ready on Sunday, won't you?" And Alex Webster was always ready. He gutted it up quite a bit.

Rick Casares was another fine fullback. He was probably the best blocking fullback of all and a great cutback fullback, too. He'd start off left tackle and then cut way over to the center. He holds all the all-time rushing records for the Chicago Bears and was just a great money ballplayer.

HALFBACK

I played three years in college against Jon Arnett when he was with Southern Cal and I was with Notre Dame, and he was the best college halfback I ever saw. He was quick, he had great balance, great speed, good hands. During his first few years in the pros with the Los Angeles Rams, he was even more dangerous than in college. But he was playing for a bad ball club and didn't get all the recognition he deserved.

Ranking with Arnett is Lenny Moore of the Baltimore Colts. In the years that the Colts were really devastating—1958 and '59 especially—Moore was the biggest halfback threat in the league. I remember one year he gained 422 yards running the ball from halfback, and 846 yards catching the ball as a flanker. That's when he was really dangerous, when he was doing both. He had, and has, a great pair of hands.

Then in 1964 when the Colts became more of a ball-control team, Moore had one of the best years running he ever had. He led the league in scoring and one touchdown he scored against us was unbelievable. He went ten yards and broke three tackles and took Jesse Whittenton into the end zone with him.

Moore has great maneuverability. He's not an overpowering kind of runner but he's fast and he glides through and changes direction so quickly. He's not hard to tackle except you think you got him and he's gone.

Among the newer halfbacks in the league, Tommy Mason of the Minnesota Vikings looks like he can be a great one. He's going good now and will be even better when his offensive line gets stronger. He's got fine balance, he's a very high stepper, and he can stop and start, stop and start very quickly.

QUARTERBACK

I think Johnny Unitas will be rated as one of the greatest quarterbacks who ever lived. His passing is absolutely unbelievable, it's so accurate. He gets set quicker than anyone I've ever seen, he gets rid of the ball quicker than anyone I've ever seen. And he knows his receivers. He's probably the best quarterback in the league at hitting his receivers on the break. He and Raymond Berry are a tremendous team. The ball will be in the air before Berry cuts. The instant he cuts, the ball is right there. And Johnny is a tough quarterback. He takes a good beating, but keeps his head about him at all times.

One of the worst things I've seen in sports happened in Baltimore one year when we were up and they were down. They introduced Unitas over the public address system and the Baltimore fans booed him. And I stood on the sidelines and I don't know who I was talking to, but I said this has got to be one of the greatest injustices in sports I've seen since I've been in the league. You know, fans forget very quickly. But Johnny Unitas will always be remembered.

Behind Unitas I would have to rank Bart Starr. I think that because of myself, and because of Jim Taylor, because of a great offensive team and because of a great defensive team over the years, that Bart hasn't received as much publicity as he should have. Every year he's in the top three in passing. If he doesn't have the fewest interceptions, he's second. And every year he's usually the top percentage throwing quarterback in the league. The last few years, his percentage of completions has been over 60 per cent.

Some people say Bart can't throw a long ball. That's a fallacy. I mean you don't have to throw the ball over sixty-five yards. You can't because you don't have that much time to tie the ball in a string for seventy yards and the guy will never be down there, anyway. And Bart can throw very accurately. He's the best short pass quarterback in the league. I don't think there's any doubt about that. He does a great job. He's a great control-type quarterback and very, very smart.

Nobody wants to win more than Bart. Nobody gets more disgusted with losing than Bart and particularly with himself. He is a very sensitive guy. There are ballplayers in football, like me, that the coach can chew out and really give constructive criticism to. There are other type ballplayers, like Bart, where you can correct their mistakes, but you can't correct them in a harsh way. Bart Starr is like that. He says, "You know, I've been in this league so many years and every time he does criticize me, chew me out, my toes burn and I can feel it all the way to my head." But Bart Starr is a man people respect and don't you believe it about nice guys finishing last.

The other top quarterback of my time was Y. A. Tittle. He was an excellent scrambling quarterback, adept at the screen, and he threw the ball very accurately. I was very happy for Y. A. when he had those great years with the Giants, because he was due; after all those years in San Francisco with a loser, he deserved more than what he had.

FLANKER

This is still a relatively new position in pro football and no one has yet stood out from the crowd, like at other positions. But there have been some good ones.

I haven't seen too much of Bobby Mitchell but what I have seen and what I have heard from other players has convinced me that Mitchell is one of the best flankers in the game. They say he doesn't have the real great hands that a pass receiver should, but he has improved year after year. He's got tremendous speed and he's very elusive and if he catches the ball out there, you better watch out or he's gone.

I think our own Boyd Dowler has a chance to be one of the great ones. He weighs 235 pounds and he can run the 100 in ten flat. He's big and strong and a fine pass catcher and he's getting better every year.

Another good one is Terry Barr of the Lions. He has exciting moves and he is very intelligent. An underrated ballplayer.

SPLIT END

I don't know of one standout but I would rate Raymond Berry, Del Shofner, Tommy McDonald, Johnny Morris, and Gail Cogdill all very close. They all have that ability of catching the football, then running with it. McDonald is probably the best runner of the group, Shofner has the best hands. Berry and Cogdill maybe combine the two elements the best (Berry has tremendous fakes) and Johnny Morris is a real clutch player.

TIGHT END

It's strictly between Mike Ditka of the Bears and Ron Kramer. Ditka seems faster than Ron though I don't know how fast he'd be in a straightaway race because sometimes Ron fools you. He runs his patterns a little slow. Ditka is more of a breakaway threat. I don't think there's a better pair of hands in football than Ron Kramer's. I don't think I've seen him drop over twenty passes that hit him in the hand since I've known him—over an eight-year period. I've seen him catch a ball—just completely engulf the ball—in one hand. He's got big hands and he's so strong from his waist up. He's immense. He weighs 250 and most of it is chest and shoulders. He's definitely one of the best blockers. I think maybe he's got a little edge over Ditka in blocking. But as far as catching the football and being a tough guy, Ditka is as tough as they come.

Ron of course is one of my favorite people. We've been very close ever since 1957 when we drove up to camp together as rookies. Ron is not only a fine football player, but he is a man of his own convictions. If he thinks one way, he's going to say it and damn the consequences. And he's a hard guy to coach mainly because he doesn't need too much coaching. But he'll give you 110 per cent and he'll play when he's hurt and he does a helluva job.

I remember when Ron came out of the service in 1960 he had an ulcer and he was down to 215 pounds. And he absolutely ate and drank the ulcer right out of his system. The doctors said no Scotch, no pizzas, no whatever. And Ron drank Scotch and martinis and ate everything he shouldn't, and the next morning he'd be drinking three bottles of Maalox and he'd be sick as a dog and the next night he'd go out and do the same damn thing. He was going to have a good time and nobody was going to stop him, and no physical thing was going to stop him. And it didn't. He got rid of his ulcer, regained his weight, and went on to become the best tight end in the business.

TACKLE AND GUARD

Some of the game's best tackles later switched to guard—Jim Parker and Forrest Gregg to name two—and the positions are almost interchangeable. But the three best tackles I've ever seen are Parker and Gregg and Roosevelt Brown of the New York Giants. Brown has always been just a tremendous blocker. Parker has weighed anywhere from 275 to 300 and he's awfully fast for his weight, an immovable object. Our own Forrest Gregg is the best offensive blocking tackle in the league. He's not oversized, a solid 255. But he's smart in technique, form, in getting the job done the right way. If he is supposed to put his head a certain way, it's there. He does it all the best.

John Gordy of the Lions has been a great guard over the years but I have to put our guards, Jerry Kramer and Fuzzy Thurston, ahead of everybody, because they paid off well for me.

In most of the plays that I ran, one was always out in front of me. If it was a trap, the left guard was trapping and the right guard was trapping going the other way. And if it was a sweep either way, both of them were in front of me pulling. If it was a trap up the middle, they'd be right in the midst of me. So one way or the other, I'm right with one of them all the time.

Jerry Kramer is just a beautiful man. He has had an unbelievably hard life. He was almost killed by an accidental shotgun blast when he was seventeen. He had a detached retina, he had a sliver go through his abdomen and almost come out of his back, he had a leg fracture that parted the tibia and fibula at the base where they are joined. He has had more bad injuries in football than anyone I know. And he was out almost all of 1964 with abscesses in the abdomen that have required three different operations. He is such a thoughtful guy and everyone is pulling for him to play again.

When I was unable to kick field goals in 1962 because of a knee injury, Jerry moved right in and kicked brilliantly. And in 1964 when I was trying to regain my kicking form, Jerry was out with me looking for things I was doing wrong, and encouraging me when I was down. He told a writer early that season, "I think our trouble was we expected too much when Hornung returned from his suspension. We felt, 'The Horn's back, nothing to worry about.' And we subconsciously let up just a little." Jerry's that kind of guy.

Fuzzy is quite the opposite of Jerry. He is a fun-loving guy off the field and a monster on. He has probably got the greatest recuperative powers of anybody I've seen. He played over a hundred straight games and that's pretty good, especially when you're playing line.

Fuzzy enjoys nothing more than making me feel like six inches. He is fond of dedicating songs to me. "I want to sing this song for Paul," he says—"Just a Gigolo." Or, "Now for the song Hornung sings to all waitresses and WACs the country over—'To Spend One Night with You.'" And he has introduced me at formal dinners like this: "Tonight we are favored by having with us the great Paul Hornung—and he wears boxer shorts." But I still love him.

CENTER

I never see the offensive films so I am going by what the defensive players tell me. About Jim Ringo, who played with us until 1964, they tell me he's the best. I've got to believe it.

Jim is real quick and a very good cut blocker, cutting the middle linebacker so quick. And he's off the ball faster than anyone on the offensive line, even though he has to snap the ball. He'd sidestep just like a guy starting off.

Behind Ringo, I would rate Ray Wietecha of the New York Giants and Dick Syzmanski of the Baltimore Colts, both underrated performers.

That's the offensive team. The defensive team I can speak a little more personally about because every one of the guys I mention—not counting my teammates—has given me trouble at one time or other.

END AND TACKLE

Individually, we may not have had the best defensive ends and defensive tackles in pro football, but in one period I think the Packers had the best four defensive linemen in football playing together—Willie Davis and Bill Quinlan at ends, Henry Jordan and Dave Hanner at tackles. On one side we had Quinlan, who never rushed the passer but was the best end over a period of years I've ever seen against the trap. The way he worked to counter the trap was to try and jam the hole. If the guard pulled out, Quinlan would answer not by going for the back, but going for the guard. He would try to hit the guard and try to stop him right there in the hole, and jam up the hole. Quinlan was a master at this.

Playing alongside Quinny was Henry Jordan, who has always been great on the pass rush. Jordan at 240 has done more with less weight than anybody in the league. He is the quickest defensive tackle in the league; he can run the 100 in maybe eleven seconds flat. And he has great ability with his hands to get rid of a blocker.

On the other side we had Dave Hanner, who played the traps, who would kind of sit and wait, and Willie Davis, who would run around and get the passer. Hawg Hanner was tough and unbelievably strong. He was always kidding that I was going to whip him before he retired. But if I ever gave him a shot in the head or something, then I'd run. I wouldn't stay close with him. Because when he fools with you, you think he's kidding around and he almost breaks your arm off. Dave never goes out at night and he's always in bed at ten o'clock and he's the first one up on the team. In the training camp he always comes down and wakes you up, like he'll throw a bucket of water in your face; or, if you're sound asleep, he'll just pick you up and carry you around until you wake.

Willie Davis we call Dr. Feelgood. There was a song about Dr. Feelgood one time and Willie's personality fits that piece. He always feels good, you know. He's got a great gift of gab. He's very funny and everyone loves to hear him tell a story. He can tell a story about walking into a grocery store and have you in stitches. And down on the field, he's just a tremendous pass rusher.

So we had two guys who were definitely top pass rushers —one on the left and one on the right—and two guys, one on the left and one on the right, who were great against the run. And that's one of the reasons our defense was so tough over the years.

But the best defensive end I've ever seen was Gino Marchetti of the Colts. Gino had a lot of range and he was very quick and very durable. I saw him at times, even when the offensive tackle blocked him perfectly, still get his hands on the quarterback.

The toughest defensive end of all to cut down on a sweep was Doug Atkins of the Bears. At six feet eight, 260 pounds, he had to be the strongest sonofagun the league has ever seen. When he made up his mind to get the quarterback, you were going to have to put three guys on him. And if you tried to cut him—and this is the only way you're going to get these defensive ends down on a sweep—Atkins would jump right over you. He scissored right over you. A couple of times he never touched me. He just jumped right over me. Sometimes you just hoped to catch his feet on the way down, knock him off balance. But there was no one way you could hit him in the shoulders and try to block him—he'd knock your feet back. So when you hit him, the best you could hope for was a standoff, with the back slipping by. And the way to do this, the only way to block him, was to get a jump on the count. Cheat up close to him and get to him before he took the two steps. I think I've gotten more of a kick out of blocking him the couple of times I managed to, than I ever have from anybody.

The other great defensive end was Andy Robustelli of the Giants. He was also difficult to cut down on a sweep. But with Robustelli, it was finesse, not brute strength. He was the kind of guy who not only lulled the offensive tackle to sleep, but he slid off the tackle and got by with that quickness. He was a great outside rusher on the passer, a real intelligent ballplayer. He was the key to their defense. In those years that we played the Giants for the title, we thought we'd go straight at Andy because he wasn't that big. We felt we'd have a better chance going at him rather than running away from him. But he was always tough and often surprised us.

Leo Nomellini of the San Francisco 49ers is certainly one of the great all-time tackles. He was very strong and agile. Oh, he just had everything he needed. Game after game against us, he gave me an awful time.

The toughest pair of defensive tackles in the league are the Lions' Roger Brown and Alex Karras. Jerry Kramer always said Karras was the toughest he ever faced, and Fuzzy always said Brown was the toughest he ever faced. Brown weighs 300 pounds and is as strong as a bull and Fuzzy just took more of a physical beating playing against him than he did against anyone else.

One day a few years ago Jim Taylor was aggravating Brown. Jimmy in those days had a habit of hollering and screaming at the defensive guys, kicking and making use of his elbow. And he was giving Brown a little trouble and Fuzzy came back and grabbed Taylor and said, "Hey, you lay off that sonofagun. I gotta block him every time. Don't you dare get him mad."

Two of the best young tackles in the league now are Merlin Olsen of the Rams and Bob Lilly of the Dallas Cowboys. Olsen is big, strong, and fast and Lilly has great range and he's very quick, too.

I shouldn't forget a couple of other men, too, who are now dead.

In my first couple of years the Colts were pretty strong and Big Daddy Lipscomb kind of amazed me he was so big and so quick, and he could run so well.

Cal Jones of the University of Iowa was absolutely the best college lineman I ever faced, and I had to face him three years. He was big and he was quick and he was always all over the place. Cal played Canadian football after getting out of Iowa and then he was killed in an airplane accident. He was just a great, great ballplayer.

MIDDLE LINEBACKER

The best middle linebacker I played against was Joe Schmidt of the Detroit Lions. He was so quick and he was the surest tackler I've ever seen. All linebackers are tough meeting you in the hole but when you give a linebacker four or five yards' daylight, you can usually get away from them. But not Schmidt. He put his eyes right on your belt buckle and he stayed with you. I can remember, we'd run a sweep to the right and here was Schmidt, making the tackle. "Come on, Paul, come on, Paul," he would say. I could hear him waiting, just waiting, like a cat.

Bill George of the Bears was as important to the Bears' defense as Schmidt was to the Lions. He was a little different than Schmidt. The Lions played a standard 4–3 defense. The Bears played varied defenses and you were liable to see George move into defensive tackle or defensive end. He could play in the line or out of the line—he was very quick. One great trick that he had. He'd get right over the center and watch the ball. He had one hand on the ground and one hand poised. And the center would start to move the ball and George would reach up and grab it before he could finish his snap. That's how quick Bill George was.

Ray Nitschke of the Packers is just really coming into his strength. He hits harder than anybody I've ever seen. He likes it, he loves to hit. His first couple of years he wasn't married and he wasn't playing much and he got disgusted and he was hard to live with. You didn't want to be around him. He wanted to fight with his own ballplayers at the drop of a harmless crack. But he got married and quit drinking and he adopted a little boy and he settled down. He absolutely turned into a gentleman and it made all the change in the world. And he turned into a real great football player.

Sam Huff, no matter what's been said about him being overrated, was still a fine linebacker. He might be on top of the pile or underneath the pile, but he was still there.

And you've got to hand it to a guy like Chuck Bednarik. When I came into the league he was already an old-timer, and he was still just a mountain of strength. In the 1960 championship game, he was thirty-five, in his thirteenth year, and he played both ways for the Eagles against us—middle linebacker and offensive center. And he did a helluva job. He's got to be one of the all-time great linebackers.

OUTSIDE LINEBACKERS

Joe Fortunato of the Chicago Bears was the best corner linebacker against the run that I've ever seen, and Bill Forester of the Packers was the best against the pass. Forester always made All-Pro but he was the most underrated All-Pro in the league. He was very quick and covered outside well, and when he had to cover underneath an end (with the flanker out to the left, he would go out to try to stop the square-out) he got back better than anyone I've ever seen.

Dan Currie, who played with the Packers from 1958 through the 1964 season, was maybe the best all-around linebacker. Dapper was very, very intelligent. He didn't make the big mistakes and he was always in the right spot at the right time and followed his keys very well. He was real strong. He was also a fun guy who liked to have a good time and I'll miss him in Green Bay. Dapper loved his beer and hated to be home and that's why we called him, "Street." Because he loved to get on the street. He would say, "I couldn't get to sleep last night. I knew you were all out on the street." And we nicknamed his two boys, "Street" and "Sidewalk."

DEFENSIVE BACKS

Corner back is probably the hardest job in football to
play and it usually takes five or six years' experience before
you're a professional. So much depends on individual ability. It's like our corner back, Jesse Whittenton, said when
Coach hollered at him because somebody beat him. "Well,
what's he expect," Jesse said. "Does he expect a twelve-
thousand-dollar defensive back to cover a twenty-five-thou-
sand-dollar end?"

Jesse over the years has been one of the best corner backs.
Few passes have been thrown to his side, and that's because the other teams respected him. Jesse used to be a
wild and uninhibited Texan. But he's more serious now.
He's married and owns a restaurant in Green Bay and he's
at a point in life where he realizes all the fooling around's
over and let's get down to work.

Herb Adderley, our other corner back, is a great natural
athlete. He's real quick. I think he could be one of the fast-
est men in the league, but he just runs fast enough to beat
the next guy. He runs like he's gliding—he just glides along.
And he's got lots of big years ahead of him.

Some defensive backs get more publicity than others, the
ones who are great punt-returners and kickoff-return men.
Abe Woodson is one. He's always been a great corner back
but he's considered an even greater corner back as far as the
fans are concerned because he's such a great kickoff-return
and punt-return man. When you ask fans, who's the best
corner back, they'll say Woodson. And they're actually
thinking about punt returns and kickoff returns.

Woodson isn't the best but he's one of the best. He's quick
as a cat. I played with him in the college All-Star game and
a couple of other games and I felt then he probably had the
greatest running potential I've ever seen. I think he could

have been one of the finest offensive halfbacks in the league if they had played him there.

But the finest corner back I've ever seen was Night Train Lane of the Lions. Lane might get beat for the big one, but he'd be in your hair all day long. On runs, he came up real quick and was a sure tackler. He was fast as hell, with great reactions. Over the years he was probably the best outside corner back in the league.

As for safeties, Jimmy Patton of the Giants was always a real fine safetyman in their defense. He always played a key defense where they had a free safety, and Jimmy was the free safety. I've seen Jimmy from an off-side safety break up a fly pattern. If, say, Unitas were throwing the bomb to the right end down the right, and Patton was left safety, he'd go way over and get the ball. He had great reactions.

This youngster with the Bears, Roosevelt Taylor, is probably the best tackling safety I've ever seen. He's a superb pass defender. He's very quick. He can get beat and still catch up to you. But he'll stop all the sweeps. He'll tackle you on the line of scrimmage, even if he has to come all the way over to the other side.

Our Willie Wood is going to be a top safety, too. He's amazing. He came to us as a free agent. Nobody wanted him. He is very fast and has very quick reactions and guards well against passes, and he's always in the right place at the right time, and doing the right thing. He comes up with the big play time after time. Willie makes an interception and shakes his head and says, "It's not my birthday. Why they keep giving me cakes, I don't know."

3. THE SUBJECT IS WOMEN

Palm Beach . . . Hartford, Connecticut . . . Washington . . . Honolulu . . . Coral Gables . . . San Francisco . . . Escanaba, Michigan . . . Chicago . . . Nashville . . . Cleveland . . . Chicago . . . Paris, France . . . Chicago . . . East Point, Georgia . . . St. Louis . . . Dallas . . . Atlanta . . . Menasha, Wisconsin . . . Hollywood . . . Hollywood, California . . . Hollywood . . . Worcester, Massachusetts . . . Hollywood . . . Hollywood . . . Evanston . . . Toronto, Canada . . . New York . . . Indianapolis . . . Baton Rouge . . . New York City . . . Louisville . . . Nashville . . . Miami . . . Lexington . . . Cincinnati, Ohio . . . Louisville . . . Louisville . . . Chicago . . . Miami . . . Charlotte, North Carolina . . . Indianapolis . . . Miami . . . Dallas, Texas . . . New Orleans . . . Chicago . . . Burbank, California . . . Hollywood . . . Arlington, Virginia . . . Denver, Colorado . . . Columbus, Ohio . . . Hollywood.

The little black book for 1963.

I have one for every year. After you've been around the National Football League for three or four years, you naturally have your little book. When I was in college I had the greatest little black book in the world—alphabetical, by the numbers, rating system, the whole bit. And somebody stole the damn thing on me.

The little black book comes in handy when I haven't been in a city for a year or so. I find myself forgetting names easily so I just get this little book out and look in and call the numbers and see if they're still there. Lots of them I keep in touch with, the ones I really dig.

And if I don't keep in touch with them, they usually keep in touch with me. Like in Green Bay during the season, I may get three or four calls a night from girls. Either they want to come up—and see me sometime, as Mae West would say—or they just want to talk, renew a friendship.

One night in the fall of 1964 when I was lying on the couch trying to rest the pinched nerve in my neck, I got this long-distance call from Richmond, Virginia. Here's a one-sided version of the conversation.

"Sure, I'm well. No, I'm not. I got a bad neck. . . . No, it's not real bad. . . .

"How long you going to be in Richmond? . . . Then you'll come and see me? . . . You like Richmond? A swinging town?

"You what? I love you, too. . . . Well, it's mutual. . . .

"I'm going to do a book and give you a whole chapter. Yeh. It'll be called, 'Marilyn Monroe II.' . . . Why? You lost weight? . . .

"Of course I want to see you. Whenever you get enough money to come and see me, I want you to come. . . . I can't afford to pay your way. If I paid your way, I'd feel kind of guilty about it, you know that. You what? Oh, well you want me to reimburse you? Hey, no chance, no chance. . . . Why don't you hop a plane and come up today?

"Oh, I was in love with you once. Yes, I was. No, there will always be something there between you and me, you know that. . . . Huh? I don't know. I haven't seen you. I don't get to see you that much any more.

"I'll be home in December, darling. About the sixteenth.

Until Christmas. . . . Well, after that I'll be home all year.
. . . You know, there's a couple of things I got to do. . . .

"Listen, give me your number where I can call you there.
. . . What've you got, an apartment there?

"Sure, you can come and see me. Make it during the week,
though. I'm booked up on the weekends (laughter). What?
I got to work on the weekends. . . . Huh? I'm just kidding
you, honey. I just want to see you. When would you like to
come? Well, get yourself on the plane. Huh? All right. . . .

"Honey, we're going to Frisco this week. . . . Friday.
You can come up Wednesday and Thursday. . . .

"All right, we'll go right after the season. We'll go to Jamaica. . . . Sure, I will.

"Of course I still love you. No, I'm just tired. You know
I can never stay on the phone over three minutes. And this
is five. I'll talk to you. . . . Get up here, you hear? . . .
All right, honey, bye, bye."

Translated: I used to see this girl once in a while and she
looks just like Marilyn Monroe and she called me with half
a mind to come up and see me, but I wasn't about to en-
courage her, and I told her I'd see her after the season.
Which I did. We didn't go to Jamaica together. We met in
New York.

A fairly typical phone conversation. The big standing joke
in Green Bay used to be—Who's Hornung going to have in
this week? I would import girls in every week, from Chicago, New York, etc. But in 1964, the year of my return to
football, I didn't do it. I knew it would be a hectic year and
I was more serious about things.

And that, I think, indicates something about me. Women
have always been foremost in my thoughts—next to football.
I'm a professional football player first, a bachelor second.
And being a professional football player *and* single, there
are never any problems about finding girls.

They call me on the phone like that fiancée from Richmond, and if they don't call, they write. Some of the letters I get are pretty preposterous. Like I got one from a boy who asked for an autographed picture and there was this "P.S." on it:

"I would like to have one, too. I am Jimmy's aunt. I just love big men. Why don't you just come with it."

And another one from a girl of sixteen:

"Dear Paul, I love you and the Packers very much. I love you and the boys more than the Beatles. I think they're fat. . . ."

A lot of times the girls write and enclose a picture. Usually, they try to be subtle, like this one:

"Dear Paul Hornung, my mother has been a fan of yours since your green Golden Boy days at Notre Dame. I'm going home at Thanksgiving and I would like to take her an autographed picture of you. Of course, I thought it only fair to send you my picture in return."

I never pay any attention to this type of letter, unless the picture is of an exceptionally good-looking girl. I never will forget a letter I got from a girl in Pennsylvania. She sent her picture along and I'll be damned if she wasn't Brigitte Bardot No. 2. She put in a couple of pictures, in fact, one in a low-cut dress, another in a bathing suit. She said, "You're real cute and I'm a pro football fan and I'd like to meet you." I'm always a little bit leery of this kind of letter. Usually, I don't want to meet anybody who writes a letter like that. But this girl was an exception, she was just a flat knockout. So I jotted down her number in my book.

Then I was in Pennsylvania for a banquet and I called her. She drove up and it turned out it wasn't the same girl as the picture. She wasn't bad but I was expecting Brigitte Bardot, you know. She must have had a little intestinal fortitude just to show up. I asked her about the picture and she said, "Well, that was taken a couple of years ago when I was modeling real well." So we had coffee and I said sayonara.

Guys have come up to me and said, "What's the secret of your success?" And there isn't any secret. As I said, I'm a professional football player and I'm single. There are other guys in the league who are better-looking than me (though it hurts me to admit it). I remember the time I was introduced to Ben Agajanian. This was in 1961 when I went into the Army and Ben joined the team to help with the field-goal kicking. I was in the house combing my hair and staring into the mirror when Ben came in.

"This is Ben Agajanian," someone said.

I just kept on combing, kept on looking in the mirror, completely ignoring Ben. I looked at myself and said, "Gotta be the handsomest guy in the world." Ben broke up.

I've got this curly blond hair, which is mainly why they started calling me Golden Boy. And someone described me as having "clear blue eyes, dimpled chin and sensuous lips." Which is all right, even if my eyes are green. I accept it. But what I think the girls really like about me is my *charm*. I drive a Cadillac, and that's part of the charm. I like to dress well, and that spells charm. (I have maybe twenty-five suits and a dozen sports jackets, more ensembles, someone said, than Perry Como. I only *wish!*) I like to take women to the nicest places, good entertainment, and have a nice dinner. I think this is all very attractive for a girl, naturally, to take them to the nicest places and all the night spots.

And you're in these spots with different girls and you start making the columns. Within one week, I was in Winchell's column as having fallen out of love with a girl in New York, and a few days later Ed Sullivan had me falling in love with someone else. And I think that's how the reputation spreads, and it is exaggerated.

But the image builds up. During my sabbatical there were rumors around that I was going to be traded to the New York Giants for Del Shofner. Just before the Giants' playoff game in '63 with the Chicago Bears, Giant coach Allie Sherman called a team meeting.

"You've all been hearing these rumors about me trading Shofner for Hornung," Sherman said. "Well, let me tell you, I wouldn't trade Del Shofner for Paul Hornung and *all* his girl friends."

With that, Mo Modzelewski jumped up and cried, "Wait a minute, Coach. Take a vote, take a vote!"

What it is, really, is that after about eight years of traveling around, you meet a lot of people, get pretty good connections, and have no problems finding little fiancées. So it becomes—if you're going there, here's a little girl to look up. And I most always did.

The travel has been very broadening. For instance, I have worked for Jantzen since 1961 and that's given me a wonderful opportunity to go places and meet a lot of nice people. I've traveled for them to California, to Mexico, to Hawaii. My first year with Jantzen I went to Honolulu for three days. That time we won the volleyball championship of Hawaii. There was Frank Gifford and myself and one other guy who kind of helped us along, Bob Pettit. Bob is six-nine and one of the great professional basketball players of all time and he naturally scored all the points. We put him next to the net and those poor Hawaiians didn't have a chance.

In the spring of 1963 I went to Mexico for Jantzen and that was a ball. There were a lot of pretty girls there and I thought it was a great place. I enjoyed dating some of the Spanish girls. They couldn't understand me and I couldn't understand them, and it was kind of comical. Finally, I learned to say all that was necessary—*amo*—I love you.

Later on that stay we went to Acapulco and a funny thing happened to us on the way.

We were having dinner at a Hilton hotel. There was Terry Baker and myself, and a bunch of other fellows and their wives. I asked the bell captain at the hotel where was a nice place to go, a nice cocktail lounge. "Somewhere I could go if I wanted to fall in love," I said.

He gave me the name of one place and during dinner I said, "Come on, I want to buy you a drink at this real nice cocktail lounge. It's supposed to be one of the most exclusive places in Acapulco."

"What's the name of it?" someone asked.

"Casa Rebecca."

There was a short debate whether to go there or stay at the hotel. Finally, one of the fellows said, "Well, this place sounds a little more Spanish so let's go there."

We piled into three taxis and started driving. It was a rough drive. Acapulco is very hilly and the roads are rough and one of the wives in the party was about eight months' pregnant. But we finally got there.

It was an outdoor place, by the sea. There were big tables and a jukebox and a bar way in the back. We looked around and something didn't seem quite right. One of the guys took me aside and his face was pale.

"You know what this is," he said. "This is a brothel."

I said, "You got to be kidding."

Casa Rebecca, house of Rebecca. I should have known. The waiter came over and asked us if we wanted some girls. And we said sure. And we had some expensively dressed girls come over and sit down at our table.

The wives with us were all excited. "It's beautiful," they said. "We always wanted to be in one." And we stayed awhile and talked and had a couple of drinks and then left.

I liked that. I like excitement when I go out and I think

my dates like to share that. Someone once wrote that I made a trip downtown sound like a polar expedition. Which is true, in a way. You can call it a zest for life, or what have you. I just like to have a good time. I like people, I especially like girls. I enjoy their company. I would dread letting a week go by without seeing a girl, even for the companionship alone.

But I don't like to be pulled at by women. I don't like to argue with them. If I particularly like a girl, once she starts arguing, I've got to leave. I don't enjoy that at all. I just say, you know, I'm sorry, it's getting late.

Sometimes the girls can get real pushy. Like one Monday night I was in a bar in Green Bay and it was mobbed and a girl slipped through and put her hand on my arm.

"Paul," she said, "don't you remember me? I met you out on the Coast last year. You were out there for a game. I was working then. Remember?"

"I'm trying to remember," I said. But I knew damned well I had never seen that girl before in my life.

And that same night in the same place, another girl came over and asked me to sign an autograph on the white collar of the dress she was wearing. I said, "Nothing doing. Get a piece of paper and I'll give you an autograph. I'm not going to sign my name on anybody's dress."

In addition to the women, there are a lot of men in the country who want to fix you up. And sometimes there are a lot of men who really think it's something if they can introduce you and say, "This is Paul Hornung. He plays football for the Green Bay Packers." Which really makes me cringe. I would much rather they'd introduce me as Paul Hornung and forget about it. I can talk on my own. I don't need anybody to try and make points for me, for heaven's sake.

But that's not as bad as the guy who tries to make points by impersonating me. One night in 1962, during the season,

I got a call from a girl in Atlanta who was running a cabana down there.

"I hate to bother you," she said. "This is strictly business." She sounded nice so I regretted her saying that. "Have you been to Atlanta lately?"

I said, "No."

"Well," she said, "we had a guy down here who said he was you. He was blond and he was big and he walked with a limp. And we read that you had a bad knee, and we were taken. I actually fixed him up on a date."

I said, "I'm sorry about that, but next time I come to Atlanta, I'll look you up so you can know the real me."

I did, too, and this girl was tall and beautiful and we dated a couple of times.

Tall and beautiful. That's the elementary way to rate a woman. Looks and figure are naturally No. 1. I've always been ignited by a pretty figure, a pretty face. I think that after you get to know somebody a bit more, it goes a helluva lot deeper than looks and everything. I remember one girl in Hollywood who was so beautiful. Her figure was out of this world, a Miss Somebody or other from somewhere. And after a while I found she had no sense at all. After two or three dates talking with her, if you asked her who Khrushchev was, she'd be stuck for an answer. And everybody wanted to be with this girl. And I couldn't be with her. It was too boring.

You can get very bored with a dumb beauty. I like a girl to be intelligent and sharp, a good conversationalist. I'd rather maybe go out with an ugly girl and have a lot of laughs. There's a couple of plain girls that I see in Chicago, just friends. And sometimes I have a date with a fiancée and I say to these girls, come on and have dinner with us. Because they're just beautiful people to be with.

The girl thing started with me when I was very young.

We had a guy living in the Portland section of Louisville, who was the Porfirio Rubirosa of Portland, a real swashbuckler, the honcho of the block. He was a nice-looking guy and he worked in the ironworks. He had a new car at all times. He might have made $150 a week, which was a lot of money in those days, and he was single, about twenty-eight, and he had all the fiancées.

Somehow he took a liking to me and I can remember him telling me when I was twelve, "I'm going to have somebody make love to you before next year, so you can know what you're doing." I always remember that. But I never took him up on it. At that time I was too bashful to be with somebody twenty-two years old. Another two years and it would have been all right.

So he was the first influence, but then I began to do all right in my own age group. In those days we would go to a lot of house parties. And they'd turn off the lights and put on a record and they'd play what they called, "Fifteen Minutes in Heaven." You'd kiss a girl for the whole record and then they'd change the record and you'd pick out another girl and they'd turn out the lights again. You had about twelve kids in the room and they'd be sitting around all night, kissing.

Then, when I was a little older, a bunch of us would go out on Sunday afternoons to a place called the El Rancho Club. We'd have to sneak in because we were underage. They had good colored bands there and jam sessions on Sunday and we'd pile thirteen in a car and go out there and dance.

But I never had a very active love life until I became a junior in college. In high school I was really so intense about athletics that it kind of made me shy away from girls. I think at this time, when you start getting the publicity, you feel a little self-conscious. This was the first time that my name was in the paper and naturally it was a nice thing to see and I felt a sense of pride and everything, and I felt that in my own circle in high school there was a certain image to maintain. I would never go up to a girl right off if I actually wanted to meet her because I was just a little reserved about it. I guess that's all part of growing up. Sports had a lot to do with this. There were guys who didn't play sports who were more forward than I was, and it was only because I felt that I shouldn't do this, that it wasn't the right thing to do.

And it was this way even in college. I remember one Sunday afternoon I came back to the dorm and found a girl in my room, and I was as scared as I had ever been in my life.

This girl was from Fort Wayne, which is near the college, and she had written me a few letters, and I didn't know what to do with her.

"I just wanted to say hello," she said.

I was peeved. I said, "This is ridiculous."

She said, "I didn't think it was against the rules."

"Well, it's very definitely against the rules." And I hustled her out of there as fast as I could, and I never saw her again. I was no prude, mind you, but I didn't want to get kicked out of school.

And I was this way to a certain extent until I was a junior in college.

Then I started going out on banquets and I'd come back via Chicago and soon I was going to Chicago on weekends. I had met Abe Samuels, a bachelor millionaire and a rabid Notre Dame fan, and Abe kind of took me in hand. He was so good to me during this time. He was a real swinging guy himself and it was *carte blanche* for me all over Chicago. So, naturally, I was introduced to the Chez Paree when I was a junior and I started going out with one of the girls in the show. I had a beautiful time. I met a lot of the enter-tainment people, and they were real nice. Here I was, a college junior, and I might be having breakfast with Tony Bennett. Through Abe and Phil Silvers, I met Joe E. Lewis, and I got to enjoy the company of show people. The people I had met at Notre Dame were nice people, wealthy people. And they invited me to their homes for dinner. But I found I would much rather go to the Chez Paree for dinner with a girl than be the guest of honor at a dinner party given by some Notre Dame millionaire.

And I learned a lot of things in that period, a lot of things you don't find in books, or even in a college education. I think you learn a good deal more being around people than from a book. And the learning is made easier if you have the girls to go with it.

I had the girls and I started going out all over Chicago and I started making the columns, and some of the items they printed were a little too much.

One of my early years in Green Bay I was dating a little model, Pat Mowry, who had been Miss New Hampshire, and maybe I introduced her as my fiancée once too often because she must have taken it seriously. One night I was out with another date and when I got home that night, the phone was ringing.

"Paul, congratulations," this guy said.

I said, "What do you mean?"

"On your engagement."

"What the hell are you talking about?"

Then he read the item from the early-morning edition of a Chicago paper: "Paul Hornung sent Pat Mowry, former Miss New Hampshire, an engagement ring in a football for Christmas." Which was absolutely ridiculous. But Pat didn't help matters by following up with this statement: "The whole thing has made me sick. I really am in love with Paul. I mean, I haven't dated any other fellow."

Well, she called me finally and said it was her press agent who had done it, had called a radio station and they put it on as a gag, and it went over the wire services.

The same thing happened to me a few years ago. There was an item in Walter Winchell's column that I was dating Myrna Loy. Hell, I didn't even know who Myrna Loy was. Someone had to tell me she was an ex-movie actress. I had been dating a girl in Hollywood named Myrna *Ross*. Myrna Ross was twenty-three and Myrna Loy was fifty-seven.

Rounding out my college education was an ex-Notre Dame All-American and one of the biggest characters of all time in football—Ziggy Czarobski.

Ziggy was absolutely the funniest man I have ever seen. He was a showman and artist—he could have been a success in anything he wanted to do. Ziggy was one of the great tackles at Notre Dame, and Frank Leahy could never control him; Ziggy was probably the only guy Leahy was unable to control. Ziggy came from the tough Polish side of Chicago and he was God there and naturally the Chicago Cardinals drafted him. He got twenty-eight thousand dollars for signing, which was a lot of money in 1948 for a tackle. And he took the money and went down to Miami and had a ball. He left in June weighing 230 and returned in August weighing 280. And that fall he never played more than two or three plays per game for Chicago.

When I was at Notre Dame, Ziggy was the manager of the Aurora Hotel in Aurora, Illinois, and he used to throw a big dinner party every year for the seniors on the Notre Dame team. Ziggy was toastmaster, guest speaker, and entertainer—the whole thing. He was the greatest in the business. He introduced me to the word "fiancée" for girl friend. And he introduced me to other things, too.

Like he would go to a night spot and maybe Sophie Tucker would be singing, and he would walk right up on stage and take over the show. And that was a habit I got into here and there. I used to like to go up on stage when I knew the entertainers, and barbershop. Especially when my boys, the Treniers, were playing. During the season if the Treniers were playing where we were playing, I'd tell the gang, "The Treniers are in town. Let's go." And I'd get Fuzzy up on the stage and Jesse Whittenton would be playing the drums and Ron Kramer would have one of the Treniers on his shoulders and it was a real panic. They're very close to me and they call me their "white brother."

And that's the way it's always been with me since college. And now it's becoming like a revolving door. Now it seems like I have five or six girls I'm dating around the country and all of a sudden they get married and I have to start all over again. I guess I've been helpful. A guy goes with a girl three or four years and nothing happens. I date them a while and then they up and get married. At least I'm good for something.

I guess falling in love is something different to me. When I "fall in love" with a girl I don't mean literally fall in love and be married. I mean, I'm just attracted to a woman so that I want to be with her and no one else as long as it lasts. Somehow, it never lasts. Either the girl starts arguing with you, or she wants to compete with you; and there's no way in the world she can compete with you.

So the next thing to do is try these foreign women. Which I'm doing. Recently, I met a French girl in Miami and we got along splendidly and we fell half way in love. They are so different from American women. They find somebody they like and dig, they're not catty. They don't like to talk. They just like to be with you. When you light their cigarette, they light yours. This girl was a very honest girl, honest to a point I had never realized. I didn't have to tell her I was in love with her. It would have hurt her very much if I lied to her and told her I loved her. It was enough for her to know that I liked her.

Now if only she hadn't had a husband back in France.

4. YESTERDAY, TODAY, AND TOMORROW

The night I was presented with the Heisman Trophy as the outstanding college football player of the 1956 season, the man who introduced me said something I have never forgotten to this day.

He said, "The only advice I'm going to give Paul Hornung as a man is, always be yourself. Any time you ever try to be anybody but yourself, you're licked before you start."

I have, I think, always followed that advice. There's just no way I can be different than I am. But if I could, I think I'd choose to be like two men who are complete opposites to me. One is Bart Starr; the other, my Uncle Henry.

I think of all the people I've met in sports, Bart is the most ideal man of all. If I ever have any children, I'd want them to be just like Bart Starr. He doesn't drink, he doesn't smoke, and he's devoted to his wife.

During the season Max and I always went to Bart's house once a week for a Southern fried chicken dinner. Bart's wife Cherry is a lovely girl as well as a lovely cook and we're real close, and when I'm there I tell Bart, "When you get out of town I'd sure like to slip over and be with Cherry."

Bart is one in a million. He's very intelligent, a Phi Beta Kappa graduate of Alabama. He's sensitive. He doesn't hold animosity against people. He'd do anything in the world for you and he's just a guy you respect and I've always respected him.

My Uncle Henry has been much the same way. His life is so meaningful and planned. You think idealistically of the kind of life you'd like to lead and Uncle Henry leads that life. Here's a man who never lied to anybody, never cheated anybody out of a quarter, and he's been like a father to me all my life. And I'd give him my life if he needed it.

There is probably no way I could ever be like Bart or Uncle Henry. I am what I am. But if there were a way, I'd like to try.

These days I keep thinking I've had a good time all my life; I've done as much as anybody has ever done at my age, I think. I mean, I'm no millionaire. I earn $30,000 a year now playing football but I would have had to make $150,000 to live the way I've lived and seen the things I've seen. I've made all the parties and been with all the beautiful women; and people, I think, will remember me as a good football player.

And now I'm reaching an age where I've got to think about settling down. People say about me, "He'll never get married. There's no way he'll ever get married." And the married guys on the club say, "Don't worry about it—*don't* get married." But you find yourself at the other end—single and wanting to get married and have children.

I'd really love to have kids. I don't think there's anybody on our ball club that's got kids that's adored them more than I have. Like I'm closer to Fuzzy's kids than almost he is. Maybe the perfect thing for me would be not to be married and have kids. That would probably fit the mold better.

I don't think thirty or thirty-two or thirty-five is too old to get married. But I look around and I see my friends with five or six kids growing up with them, and they're young and it's a great advantage. I don't want to be sixty years old and have any son thirteen. How are you going to have anything in common?

And after football there are other things besides marriage. I've always said I'd like to live on the Riviera and clip coupons. But my real ambition is to play golf four days a week, and practice the other three. Seriously, I think I'd like to continue in the promotion business with Bill King. This is exciting and something that kind of fits my personality. And I'd like to continue my relationship with Jantzen, and maybe do some work in real estate with Uncle Henry.

That's after football, but football isn't over yet. I'd like to play a few more years. I've seen a lot of ballplayers who discovered they had quit when they still had a few more years left, and to this day their life is full of regrets for those lost years. I wouldn't want to make that mistake, of quitting and not doing actually what I could have done, and then second-guessing myself.

I still get so much satisfaction out of football, like anyone in business gets satisfaction from a good deal. If I make a nice run, or a good kick, or throw a nice block or a nice pass, I feel very good about it in my heart.

And there are goals left, you know. I'd like to play on another championship team, naturally. I'd like to have a couple of more good years. I'd like to leave the game with a real good taste in my mouth. And all this is going to be tough, very tough. You only get a few chances in life to be on top. And it's much easier to come down than it is to go up. And if I am with the top club, the question then becomes, will I play or not, and will I have a good year, and will I escape injuries, and will the luck and the breaks stay with me?

They have, up to now. I feel I've been very fortunate. There haven't been many goals that I went after that I didn't make. When I was in high school, I wanted to play on a winning football team and make All-State. And I did both. At Notre Dame I thought of being an All-American. And when I was named No. 1 college football player in the country, I was more than fulfilled. And when I went into pro football I wanted to play on a championship team and I wanted to be the best. And both things came to me.

Naturally, if I had to do it all over again, I wouldn't have bet. I'd change that. Outside of the betting and a few injuries, which you have to expect in this game, I would change nothing. A lot of people have said about me, "Paul Hornung was born to be a winner. No matter what happens, things will always turn out right for Golden Boy." Well, the thing of it is, that was yesterday, and yesterday is over with. And the only thing I can look forward to is tomorrow. And that always poses another problem. But I'll take the same amount of luck that I've had so far out of life.